HMH | English 3D™

ISSUES

COURSE A • VOLUME 2

Printed in the U.S.A.

ISBN 978-0-358-60950-6

4 5 6 7 8 9 10   0868   29 28 27 26 25 24 23

4500864992   rX.XX

TABLE OF CONTENTS

How much SCHOOLWORK should follow you HOME?

You've probably complained about your homework before: there's too much, it's too boring, and it's ruining your weekend. You're not alone. Many students say they receive too much homework.

Having too much homework can keep students from participating in sports, academic clubs, and other after-school activities. And more time on homework means less time to spend with family and friends.

However, homework is an important part of learning. Homework helps students practice skills outside of the classroom. And teachers use homework to understand what their students have learned and what they need more help with.

Which is it: Too much homework? Or not enough?

Many teachers believe that homework is an important part of learning. But how much homework is too much?

Time for Homework ·····················

Experts recommend a maximum of 40 minutes of homework for fourth graders and 50 minutes of homework for fifth graders each night.

(Source: The National Parent-Teacher Association, 2014)

A New Normal ·····················

The number of nine-year-olds **assigned** homework increased from 65% in 1984 to 78% in 2012.

On a typical school night, 17% of nine-year-olds report having an hour or more of homework.

(Source: National Assessment of Educational Progress, 2012)

Homework Help ·····················

Close to 93% of elementary school students said their parents know how to help them with homework.

Only 53% of elementary school students said their schools provided before- and after-school homework programs.

(Source: The Survey of the American Teacher, 2011)

Rethinking Homework

American students spend more time than ever on homework. If schools lighten the load, will kids still make the grade?

by **Brenda Iasevoli** from *TIME for Kids*

One Sunday night last year, fourth grader Jackson Berg was lying in bed. Suddenly, he sat up. "I forgot to do my homework!" he exclaimed. He would have to get up early to do math problems.

Jackson is not the only one with homework troubles. US kids are hitting the books after school longer than ever. In 2004, the University of Michigan did a survey of 2,900 students. The results

Some teachers worry that a light workload will put students at a disadvantage.

showed that in 1981, nine- to eleven-year-olds spent two hours and 24 minutes on homework each week. By 2002, the amount of time spent on homework was three hours and 15 minutes. That amount only seems to be growing.

A Lighter Load

Some school districts are telling kids to put down their pencils when the bell rings. Pleasanton Unified School District, in California, is one. Its new homework **policy** took effect in September 2014. Students in kindergarten through fifth grade no longer have homework on weekends. Weeknight homework is **limited** to 30 minutes for second and third graders, and 50 minutes for fourth and fifth graders. **Assignments**

Debate:

Is 90 minutes of homework a night too much for kids? Here's what two student reporters think.

Yes!

Ninety minutes of homework is too much for fourth or fifth graders! Some experts point out that a lot of homework does not necessarily translate to higher grades. Harris Cooper, a professor at Duke University, has said there is no real proof that kids learn from most of the homework they get in elementary school.

Also, kids have after-school activities that take up much of the evening. It is good to have a **balance** between school and other activities, such as sports and playing with friends.

Michael Tobin, Oregon

No!

I think 90 minutes of homework each night fits perfectly for fourth and fifth graders. In those grades, you learn several subjects at the same time. Ninety minutes is an **appropriate** amount of time to review everything. It will help you get good grades and be prepared.

Plus, 90 minutes of homework is actually not that long. It includes reading, which many kids enjoy! Also, switching from one **assignment** to another will be interesting. Kids won't even realize that the time is passing by.

Anuva Goel, New Jersey

during vacations and holidays are discouraged.

Jane Golden is the Director of Curriculum for the 14,500-student district. "We're seeking **balance** for our children," she told *TIME for Kids.*

The Homework Battle

Some teachers argue that homework prepares kids for state tests and for college.

They worry that a lighter load will put kids at a disadvantage.

Harris Cooper is a homework expert at Duke University. He says research shows that in the elementary grades, homework has little effect on **achievement**. He believes **assignments** should be kept short. "When kids get tired, they turn off," he says.

Students in the Pleasanton school district say the new

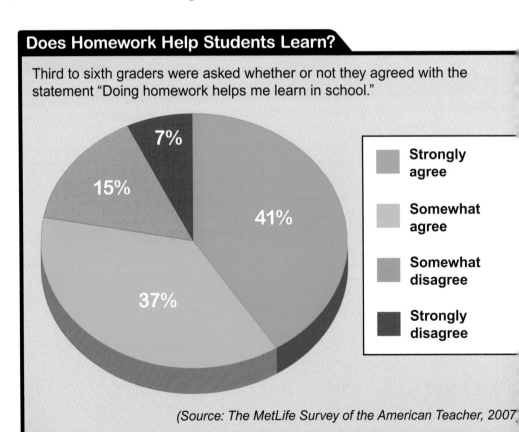

Does Homework Help Students Learn?

Third to sixth graders were asked whether or not they agreed with the statement "Doing homework helps me learn in school."

7%

15%

41%

37%

- Strongly agree
- Somewhat agree
- Somewhat disagree
- Strongly disagree

(Source: The MetLife Survey of the American Teacher, 2007

homework **policy** works. Fourth grader Noah Lee does his homework right away. Then he practices the cello, piano, and guitar. He even has time to play football. "I don't have so much homework that I can't do the things I love," he says.

Jackson Berg's school is in Dublin, California, a town close to Pleasanton. His homework load hasn't changed. "The good part," says his dad, Jacob Berg, "is that teachers are finally talking about how much homework is the right amount."

Health CONTENT CONNECTION

A lot of things can make you sick: germs, a bad diet, not washing your hands. But what about homework? According to studies, too much homework can affect your health and your brain. How? When a student has too much homework, he or she becomes stressed out. Stress slows both the body and the mind. In fact, doctors say that constant stress can damage—and even shrink—parts of the brain related to memory.

Stress can lead to other problems too, such as sleeplessness. Lack of sleep leaves the body weak and unable to fight disease. And studies show that tired students have a hard time understanding new material taught in class. If too much homework leads to stress, it may stop students from doing what they're supposed to do—learn!

TAKE A STAND

Should we cut back on homework for our health?

Debate

Are young athletes *heading* into danger?

Athletes are no strangers to bumps, bruises, and broken bones. But getting hit in the head during a game can lead to a bigger problem: a concussion. A concussion happens when your brain shakes inside your skull. It can cause headaches and dizziness. For some players, getting better can take months or years.

Some sports teams are changing the way young athletes practice and play to protect their players. One youth football league has rules against tackling. Some soccer teams don't allow young players to head the ball. Athletes who get hit hard have to sit out.

Is this enough to protect young athletes' brains? Let's tackle the evidence and find out.

Playing sports is a fun way to exercise and stay healthy. But it can also lead to life-changing injuries. Do you know the risks?

A Never-Ending Injury

For 10% to 20% of young concussion victims, **symptoms** last longer than 2 weeks. Some **symptoms** can last for years.

(Source: Institute of Medicine & National Research Council, 2014)

Head Banging

A child visits an emergency room for a sports-related concussion every 3 minutes.

Concussions make up 19% of sports-related **injuries** for athletes 8–11 years old.

(Source: Safe Kids Worldwide, 2013)

On the Field

The American Youth Soccer Organization (AYSO) does not recommend heading the ball for players under the age of 10.

The AYSO also suggests learning how to head using a soft foam ball instead of a real soccer ball.

(Source: American Youth Soccer Organization, 2014)

Hard Knocks

Football leagues set new rules to protect players from head injuries.

by Laura Modigliani from *Scholastic News*

December 8, 2011: Quarterback Colt McCoy of the Cleveland Browns was on the run. He was trying to lead his team to victory against the Pittsburgh Steelers. Just as McCoy threw a pass, Pittsburgh's James Harrison launched into him headfirst. The hit snapped McCoy's head backward. It knocked him flat on his back. A dazed McCoy had to be helped off the field. He had suffered a concussion. A concussion is an **injury** caused by a blow to the head or body that shakes the brain inside the skull.

Concussions have long been common in football. For years, they were considered part of the game. But recent studies have shown a link between concussions and long-term brain damage. To make football safer, leagues for players of all ages have set tougher rules to **prevent** head **injuries**.

Playing It Safe

In the National Football League, hits to the head or neck are illegal. Harrison had to sit out one game without pay for his brutal hit on McCoy. The **injury** forced McCoy to miss the final three games of the season.

It's not just the pros who are getting banged up. Each year, at least 140,000 kids and teens sustain concussions playing football. Research shows that most of those **injuries** happen in practice, not games. So starting in fall 2012, Pop

Warner football changed how players practice.

Pop Warner is the country's largest football organization for kids. It has almost 300,000 players nationwide. Its teams no longer spend more than one-third of their practice time on tackling and blocking. To cut down on full-speed collisions, players can't take a running start and smash into each other during drills.

Preventing head **injuries** in children is especially important because their brains aren't fully developed.

"We think that kids' brains are more sensitive to hard hits, which can cause concussions," says Dr. Julian Bailes. He's an adviser for Pop Warner. Bailes thinks the new rules may cut concussions among Pop Warner players by at least 60 percent.

Hidden Danger

A big part of the problem is that concussions are hard

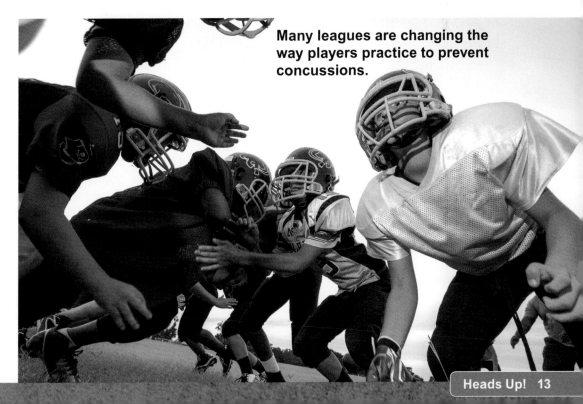

Many leagues are changing the way players practice to prevent concussions.

to detect. You can't see a concussion the way you can see other **injuries**. There are often no visible signs, like blood or bruises. So it's important for kids to recognize the **symptoms**. Bailes says that any big blow to the head can be serious. Kids who have been hit should stop playing. Then they should tell a coach or parent.

Like any body part, your brain needs time to heal after an **injury**. Players who return to action too soon risk getting more concussions. That could lead to long-term problems like permanent memory loss. So kids who are unsure about whether they've suffered a concussion should play it safe. Bailes says kids should follow this simple rule: when in doubt, sit out.

Inside a Concussion

Here's what happens to the brain when an athlete gets hit in the head:

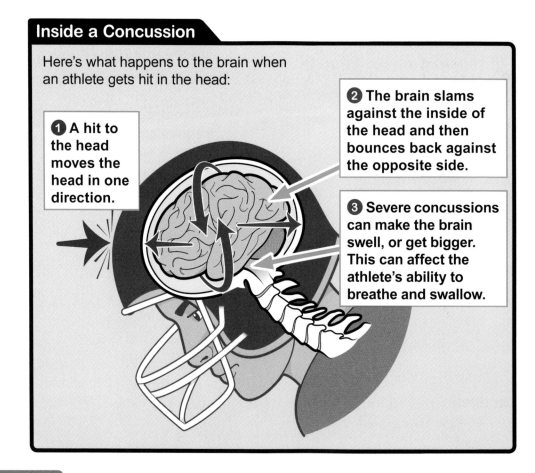

❶ A hit to the head moves the head in one direction.

❷ The brain slams against the inside of the head and then bounces back against the opposite side.

❸ Severe concussions can make the brain swell, or get bigger. This can affect the athlete's ability to breathe and swallow.

The Invisible Injury

Young athletes are at risk of suffering concussions, brain injuries that need to be treated with caution and care.

by Sean McCollum from *Scholastic Choices*

Playing goalkeeper for her soccer team, Christin Anderson ran to cut off a pass during a game. As she slid down and smothered the ball, a player on the opposing team took a swipe at it. The player's foot slammed into the back of Christin's head.

She shook off the hit and finished the game. "My vision was a little blurry. And I felt dizzy," Christin tells *Choices*. "But I didn't feel the long-term effects right away. It probably took a week and a half to realize the extent of my **injury**."

Christin started experiencing headaches and dizziness. "My balance was completely off," she says. "If I was standing and somebody bumped me, I would fall."

Christin got a concussion after she got kicked in the head by another player.

❶ Struggling in School

The effects weren't just physical. Christin was an honor student at Bloom-Carroll High School in Lancaster, Ohio. But after the concussion, she began struggling with her studies. Most alarming, her reading **ability** dropped to a third-grade level. "I'd read a paragraph and couldn't remember what I had just read," she says.

Christin was suffering from the effects of a concussion.

Most alarming, her reading ability dropped to a third-grade level.

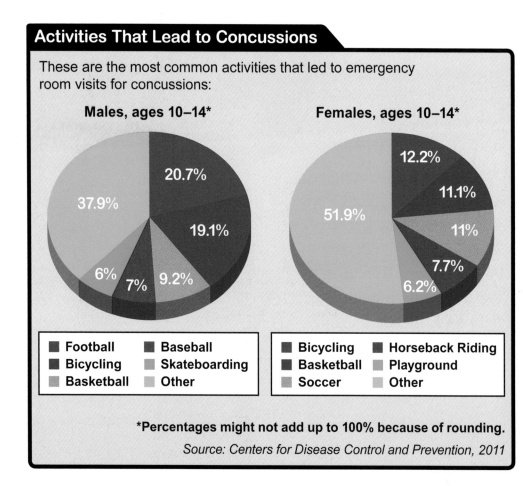

Activities That Lead to Concussions

These are the most common activities that led to emergency room visits for concussions:

Males, ages 10–14*

- 20.7%
- 19.1%
- 37.9%
- 6%
- 7%
- 9.2%

Legend:
- ■ Football
- ■ Bicycling
- ■ Basketball
- ■ Baseball
- ■ Skateboarding
- ■ Other

Females, ages 10–14*

- 12.2%
- 11.1%
- 11%
- 7.7%
- 6.2%
- 51.9%

Legend:
- ■ Bicycling
- ■ Basketball
- ■ Soccer
- ■ Horseback Riding
- ■ Playground
- ■ Other

***Percentages might not add up to 100% because of rounding.**

Source: Centers for Disease Control and Prevention, 2011

Concussions **occur** when a person receives a forceful hit to the head or upper body. The blow shakes the brain in the skull. It's like a yolk sloshing around inside an eggshell, according to Dr. Michael Collins. Collins is the Assistant Director of the University of Pittsburgh Medical Center's (UPMC) Sports Medicine Concussion Program.

At least 300,000 sports-related concussions **occur** in the United States each year, reports the Centers for Disease Control and Prevention. Christin's condition frightened her. "I was scared beyond belief," she says. She had reason to be. If not diagnosed accurately and treated with caution, a concussion can lead to long-term health problems for the brain.

❷ *Brain Drain*

Concussions can be hard to **identify**. Most concussions do not cause structural damage to the brain. A concussed brain is likely to appear healthy on X-rays and other medical tests. "Even if the **injury** is life threatening, the tests may very well be normal," Collins says.

> ## A concussed brain is likely to appear healthy on X-rays and other medical tests.

Research suggests that the effects of concussions add up. If while **recovering** from a concussion a person is hit again in the head, the **symptoms** he or she experiences may be worse. In serious cases, multiple concussions can result in brain damage or death.

Doctors believe that athletes who have had concussions shouldn't play until their **ability** to think clearly has returned to

The only effective way to treat a concussion is physical and mental rest.

normal levels. This may take a week, a month, a year, or even longer. "The **recovery** time is different in every case," Collins says. "But we're finding that, for kids, **recovery** takes far longer than has been previously thought."

To date, the only **effective** way to treat a concussion is physical and mental rest. "Too much studying delays **recovery**," Collins says. "You don't want to increase the brain's demand of energy."

On the Mend

Christin's concussion slowed down her life greatly.

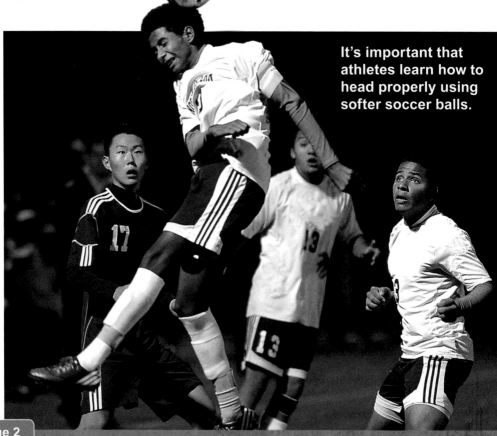

It's important that athletes learn how to head properly using softer soccer balls.

She reduced her class load during the school year and worked to catch up during summer school. She had to postpone getting her driver's license because the concussion put her at risk for having a seizure behind the wheel.

Christin, now 18, says it took almost two years for her to feel 100 percent healthy. She returned to playing goalie in soccer. But she says she played hesitantly at first. This fall, she'll attend college. She may play intramural soccer, she says.

Social Studies CONTENT CONNECTION

Return to Play Laws

In 2009, Washington state passed the first concussion-in-sports law. It was named the Zackery Lystedt Law, after a 13-year-old boy who had brain damage after getting multiple concussions while playing football. Now, every state has a law on concussions in sports for youth and/or high school students. These laws are often called Return to Play laws and include three action steps.

1. Educate coaches, parents, and athletes about concussions.

2. Remove athletes from play if they are showing the signs of a concussion.

3. Require athletes who get concussions to wait 24 hours and get permission from a doctor before returning to play.

TAKE A STAND

Should all athletes who get concussions have to wait 24 hours and get permission from a doctor before returning to play?

Debate SHOULD **ROBOTS** REPLACE **TEACHERS?**

Think about all of the work your teacher does. In the morning, your teacher takes attendance. Your teacher explains what you need to learn and grades assignments. In between, your teacher answers a number of questions on a variety of topics. Your teacher helps every student get a little bit smarter. But what if this job belonged to a robot?

Robot teachers are helping out in classrooms all over the world. They have a computer for a brain. They never get sick. And many robots can even recognize students' emotions. But how much can robots really teach us? Will they ever be as good as human teachers?

Can robots teach students better and quicker than human teachers?

Robot Jobs

About **48%** of experts believe that **robots** and other technologies will **replace** a significant number of human workers—including teachers—by **2025**.

(Source: Pew Research Center, 2014)

Robots in History

Famous artist Leonardo da Vinci drew **robot** sketches in the late 1490s—over **500 years** ago!

In **2011**, IBM developed a **robot** named Watson who beat two very smart humans on the quiz show *Jeopardy!*

(Source: Idaho Public Television, 2014)

Teaching Robots

A **2008** study looked at different types of digital instruction. It found that **robot** tutors were better than audiobooks or computers at helping children stay on task.

The same study found that the **robot** tutors improved the children's scores by at least **10%**.

(Source: Journal of Information Processing Systems, 2008)

MY NEW TEACHER, MR. ROBOT

Robot teachers are being tested in classrooms around the world. These teaching machines can instruct students in subjects such as dance, music, vocabulary, and foreign languages.

by Judith Jango-Cohen from *SuperScience*

❶ ROBOT TEACHERS HIT THE CLASSROOM

It's time for gym at a kindergarten class in South Korea. Students stretch their arms. "Up! Down! Up!" barks their gym teacher. She, or rather it, is a pink-and-black **robot** shaped like a puppy!

The **robotic** "gym teacher" is one of several types of social **robots** being tested in classrooms around the world. These teaching machines can teach students lessons in subjects such as dance, music, vocabulary, and foreign languages.

Preschool children in California learn their ABCs, colors, and shapes from a **robot** named RUBI. "The children love working with RUBI and get upset when RUBI doesn't come in," says Terrence Sejnowski. He is a neuroscientist at the University of California in San Diego who studies how humans learn.

RELATING TO ROBOTS

RUBI's relationship with its young students got off to a rocky start, however. On the **robot's** first day of school, students treated it like a toy and ripped off its arms. To solve this problem, developers **programmed** RUBI to play a crying sound when students got too rough. Now, the children hug their **mechanical** teacher instead.

> # To teach effectively, robots have to be able to read students' reactions.

This experience taught scientists an important lesson. To teach effectively, **robots** have to be able to read students' **reactions** and respond appropriately. This is because "social **interaction** is key to learning," says Dr. Sejnowski.

This type of **programming** is **complicated**. Social **robots** must be able to pick out voices from random noise. They have to identify faces and make eye contact. And most challenging of all, **robots** must know if their students understand and enjoy a lesson. They

Robot teacher Saya's face is programmed to show six different emotions.

must be able to read a child's expressions.

"As long as the **robot** passes these tests of social **interaction**, learning begins," says Dr. Sejnowski.

❷ FEARS AND CHEERS

Not all people think these **robot** instructors are a good idea. Some believe that machines should not take over an important position like teaching. They argue that

How RUBI Works

RUBI is a social robot that teaches children. The features below allow RUBI to read and respond to its environment.

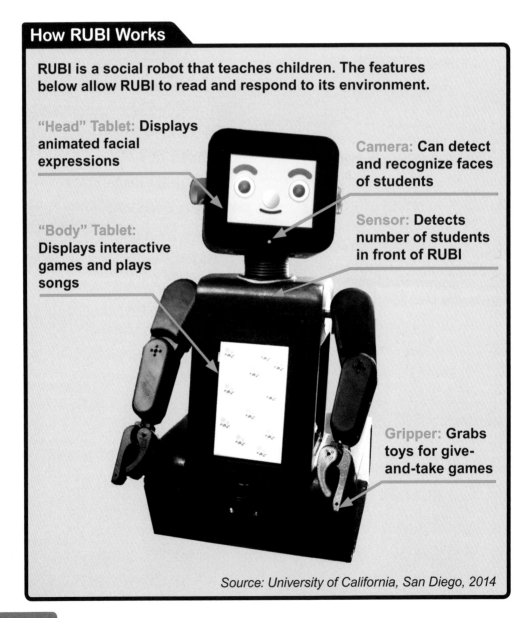

"Head" Tablet: **Displays animated facial expressions**

Camera: **Can detect and recognize faces of students**

"Body" Tablet: **Displays interactive games and plays songs**

Sensor: **Detects number of students in front of RUBI**

Gripper: **Grabs toys for give-and-take games**

Source: University of California, San Diego, 2014

people, particularly children, are unpredictable, so it's best to leave teaching to humans.

> **"The goal is for each student to have a personal robot that will become an expert on that child."**

Supporters say that social **robots** are not being **designed** to **replace** teachers. They're **designed** to assist human teachers and make learning more fun. In South Korea, where teachers are in short supply, **robots** help out with simple tasks like taking attendance. At the same time, **robots** can give children firsthand experience with advanced technology.

Robots could also automatically keep track of what students know and what they still need to learn. "The goal is for each student to have a personal **robot** that will become an expert on that child," says Dr. Sejnowski.

GRAND PLANS

Social **robots'** most important achievement may not be their classroom teaching at all. Experts say

Robots like this one can help teachers with easy jobs.

their most valuable job is helping scientists understand how children learn. This information could lead to better human teachers— teachers who are skilled at exciting children's curiosity.

To accomplish this, researchers will continue to develop better ways for **robots** and children to **interact**.

But scientists admit they have a long way to go. This is especially the case with Engkey, an English-teaching **robot** in South Korea. One student says he feels like there's something more to the machine that is his teacher. But when he told Engkey, "I love you," Engkey replied, "You need to work on your accent."

Science CONTENT CONNECTION

World Champion Robots

Each year, the Robotics Education & Competition Foundation holds a contest for middle and high school teams from all over the world. The teams design and build robots to complete a task.

In 2014, the teams had to create robots that could move different-size balls around a course. The teams had a list of building materials. They also had a short amount of time to build their robots. Working under these rules, 760 teams from 27 countries competed to see which robots would perform the best. Some of the winners received scholarships! Most importantly, everyone learned how to work together and what it takes to succeed.

This student is preparing to compete using a robot he built himself.

TAKE A STAND

Should classes in robotics be offered at every school?

THE FUN THEY HAD

by Isaac Asimov from *The Best of Isaac Asimov*

Margie even wrote about it that night in her diary. On the page headed May 17, 2157, she wrote, "Today, Tommy found a real book!"

It was a very old book. Margie's grandfather once said that when he was a little boy his grandfather told him that there was a time when all stories were printed on paper.

They turned the pages, which were yellow and crinkly, and it was awfully funny to read words that stood still instead of moving the way they were supposed to—on a screen, you know. And then, when they turned back to the page before, it had the same words on it that it had had when they read it the first time.

"Gee," said Tommy, "what a waste. When you're through with the book, you just throw it away, I guess. Our television screen must have had a million books on it and it's good for plenty more. I wouldn't throw it away."

> She was eleven and hadn't seen as many telebooks as Tommy had.

"Same with mine," said Margie. She was eleven and hadn't seen as many telebooks as Tommy had. He was thirteen.

She said, "Where did you find it?"

"In my house." He pointed without looking, because he was busy reading.

"In the attic."

"What's it about?"

"School."

Margie was scornful. "School? What's there to write about school? I hate school."

Margie always hated school, but now she hated it more than ever. The **mechanical** teacher had been giving her test after test in geography and she had been doing worse and worse until her mother had shaken her head sorrowfully and sent for the county inspector.

He was a round little man with a red face and a whole box of tools with dials and wires. He smiled at Margie and gave her an apple, then took the teacher apart. Margie had hoped he wouldn't know how to put it together again, but he knew how all right, and, after an hour or so, there it was again, large and black and ugly, with a big screen on which all the lessons were shown and the questions were asked. That wasn't so bad. The part Margie hated most was the slot where she had to put homework and test papers. She always had to write them out in a punch code they made her learn when she was six years old, and the **mechanical** teacher calculated the mark in no time.

The inspector had smiled after he was finished and patted her head. He said to her mother, "It's not the little girl's fault, Mrs. Jones. I think the geography sector was geared a little too quick. Those things happen sometimes. I've slowed it up to an average ten-year level. Actually, the overall pattern of her progress is quite satisfactory." And he patted Margie's head again.

Margie was disappointed. She had been hoping they would take the teacher away altogether. They had once taken Tommy's teacher away for nearly a month because the history sector had blanked out completely.

So she said to Tommy, "Why would anyone write about school?"

Tommy looked at her with very superior eyes. "Because it's not our kind of school, stupid. This is the old kind of school that they had hundreds and hundreds of years ago." He added loftily, pronouncing the word carefully, "*Centuries* ago."

Margie was hurt. "Well, I don't know what kind of school they had all that time ago." She read the book over his shoulder for a while, then said, "Anyway, they had a teacher."

The mechanical teacher had been giving her test after test in geography.

"Sure they had a teacher, but it wasn't a regular teacher. It was a man."

"A man? How could a man be a teacher?"

"Well, he just told the boys and girls things and gave them homework and asked them questions."

"A man isn't smart enough."

"Sure he is. My father knows as much as my teacher."

"He can't. A man can't know as much as a teacher."

"He knows almost as much, I betcha."

Margie wasn't prepared to dispute that. She said, "I wouldn't want a strange man in my house to teach me."

Tommy screamed with laughter. "You don't know much, Margie. The teachers didn't live in the house. They had a special building and all the kids went there."

"And all the kids learned the same thing?"

"Sure, if they were the same age."

"But my mother says a teacher has to be adjusted to fit the mind of each boy and girl it teaches and that each kid has to be taught differently."

"Just the same they didn't do it that way then. If you don't like it, you don't have to read the book."

"I didn't say I didn't like it," Margie said quickly. She wanted to read about those funny schools.

They weren't even half-finished when Margie's mother called, "Margie! School!"

Margie looked up. "Not yet, Mamma."

> **Margie went into the schoolroom. It was right next to her bedroom, and the mechanical teacher was on and waiting for her.**

"Now!" said Mrs. Jones. "And it's probably time for Tommy, too."

Margie said to Tommy, "Can I read the book some more with you after school?"

"Maybe," he said nonchalantly. He walked away whistling, the dusty old book tucked beneath his arm.

Margie went into the schoolroom. It was right next to her bedroom, and the **mechanical** teacher was on and waiting for her. It was always on at the same time every day except Saturday and Sunday, because her mother said little girls learned better if they learned at regular hours.

The screen was lit up, and it said: "Today's arithmetic lesson is on the addition of proper fractions. Please insert yesterday's homework in the proper slot."

Margie did so with a sigh. She was thinking about the old schools they had when her grandfather's grandfather was a little boy. All the kids from the whole neighborhood came, laughing and shouting in the schoolyard, sitting together in the schoolroom, going home together at the end of the day. They learned the same things, so they could help one another on the homework and talk about it.

And the teachers were people . . .

The **mechanical** teacher was flashing on the screen: "When we add the fractions ½ and ¼ . . ."

Margie was thinking about how the kids must have loved it in the old days. She was thinking about the fun they had.

Meet the Author

ISAAC ASIMOV

Born: January 2, 1920, in Petrovichi, Russia

Died: April 6, 1992, in Brooklyn, New York, USA

Education: Asimov graduated high school at age 15. He then attended Columbia University. There he received a bachelor of science degree, then a master's and a doctorate. He went on to teach biochemistry at the Boston University School of Medicine.

Short Stories and Books: Asimov published his first short story, "Marooned Off Vesta," in 1938. His debut novel, *Pebble in the Sky*, was published in 1950. He would go on to write nearly 500 books in all, including popular favorites *I, Robot* and the Foundation series.

Is coding the language of the future?

Behind your apps, digital devices, and computer games there's a secret language making everything work. It's called code. The people who write it are called coders.

There are many jobs available for coders. The problem is that not enough people know how to code. In America, only 1 out of 10 schools teaches students how to code. But there are other ways to learn to code, too. There are apps and online classes that make learning how to code easy and fun.

Should schools teach students how to code? Let's download some information to learn more!

We live in a digital world powered by code. Will more students learn the language of computers?

Coding Education ·······································

AP Computer Science is taught in only 5% of high schools in the United States.

(Source: The College Board, 2012)

Coding Degrees ·······································

Only 2.4% of college students graduate with a degree in computer science.

Men earn 88% of all computer science degrees.

(Source: National Science Foundation, 2009)

Coding Jobs ·······································

In 2012, about 343,700 people were employed as computer programmers.

Experts predict that 1,400,000 jobs in computing will open up from 2010–2020.

(Source: Bureau of Labor Statistics, 2012)

Cracking the Girl Code

by Eliana Docterman from *TIME for Kids*

Twenty high school girls sit hunched in front of laptops around a table at AT&T's office in New York City. Riya Satara, 17, types a series of ones and zeros to adjust a paddleball game she's designing. She's trying to make the ball follow a certain path. It's her first week learning to **code**—writing the instructions that tell a computer what to do.

Satara is attending summer camp with Girls Who Code. The national nonprofit encourages girls to enter the tech **industry**. This camp is just one of a half-dozen

Women earn only 12% of computer science degrees.

similar programs around the country offering **coding** classes for girls like Satara who have shied away from the subject. Many of the programs are supported by tech giants like Google.

"I can stand on a stage in front of 700 kids," says Satara. "But I was too scared to take a computer science class where I would have been the only girl in a room of 19 guys."

Changing that mind-set is a national challenge. By 2020, there will be 1.4 million computing jobs and not enough qualified graduates to fill them. That's why programs like Girls Who Code are trying to bring women into the **industry**. Today, only 12% of computer-science degrees go to women.

GIRLS WELCOME

Girls Who Code started in 2012 with 20 girls in one classroom. Today, the program graduates 3,000 girls from clubs and camps across the country. Founder Reshma Saujani says 95% of graduates want to major in computer science in college.

> *Today, the program graduates 3,000 girls from clubs and camps across the country.*

Educators are trying to understand how to engage girls in computer science early. Some universities are now modeling their classes after those designed by Girls Who Code, which stresses the importance of solving real-world problems. The idea is that girls are interested in helping their communities. The program also assigns group projects because research shows that girls flourish when they work as a team.

> *Currently 9 out of 10 schools in the US don't offer computer science.*

But **gender** balance won't likely be reached until **coding** becomes a part of the school day. Currently 9 out of 10 schools in the US don't offer computer science. The nonprofit Code.org aims to change that by offering **coding** classes as early as elementary school. China, Vietnam, and Britain already offer such classes.

THERE'S AN APP FOR THAT

Some developers aren't waiting for US schools to catch up. The app Hopscotch

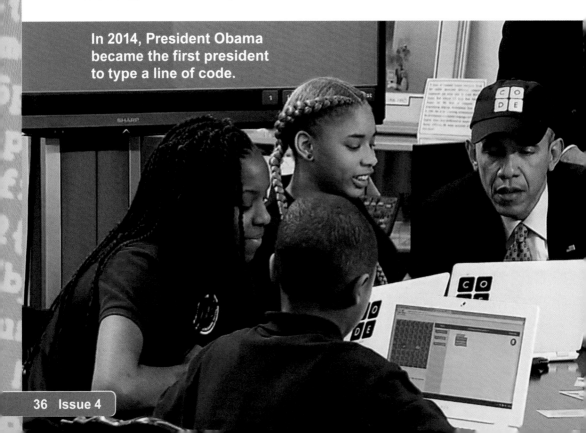

In 2014, President Obama became the first president to type a line of code.

teaches children as young as 8 years old how to build their own games with **code**. Hopscotch founder Jocelyn Leavitt says her male friends taught themselves programming when they were kids. They played sports- or war-themed video games and then re-created them.

"We wanted to tap into that desire to create something but make it more accessible to both boys and girls," she says.

So far it's a hit. More than 1.5 million projects have been **coded** with Hopscotch in the past year, about half by girls.

Riya Satara says if she'd learned **coding** earlier, she wouldn't have thought it was just for boys. Now she wants to spread her enthusiasm for tech by starting a Girls Who Code club at her school. And she's finally enrolling in a computer science class—at the advanced level.

The Job-Student Gap

There are many more computer science jobs than there are students to fill them.

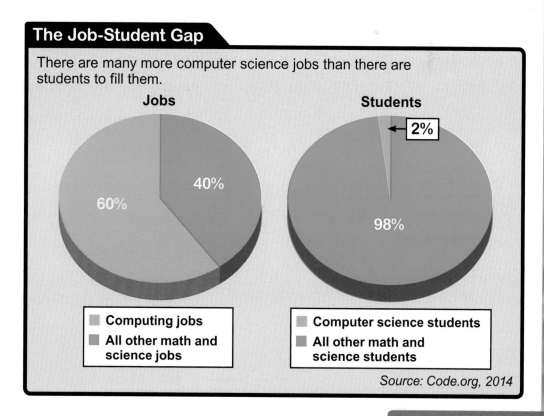

Jobs
- 60%
- 40%

■ Computing jobs
■ All other math and science jobs

Students
- 98%
- 2%

■ Computer science students
■ All other math and science students

Source: Code.org, 2014

Teaching Code in the Classroom

from *The New York Times*

1 CON: Teaching Coding to Kids Is a Scam

by John Dvorak, Technology Writer

A child should be developing basic human skills. So-called "computational thinking" is not one of them.

A second grader should be running around, throwing a ball, scratching out drawings, learning fine motor skills, and developing normal interpersonal social skills. Being hunched over a computer screen **coding** in some kiddy language to supposedly develop computer literacy is insane.

> *Computers do not belong in the classroom; they belong in the library, the home, the office.*

Let's look at what and who is behind this idea that little kids should learn to **code**. There is some direct connection to the computer **industry**, and the game of that business is to sell more and more computers. So let's load up the schools with machines.

These kids ultimately end up spending time posting pics on Facebook, giggling over online gossip, and watching cat videos. All these things are a waste of time and pathetic.

If you want to see the cause of **declining** academic achievement in American schools, look no further than the encroachment of computers into the classroom. As computers have increased, scores have **declined**. Does anyone notice this? It does not seem like much of a **coincidence** to me.

Computers do not belong in the classroom; they belong in the library, the home, the office. They do not belong in an elementary school, once called a "grammar school" for a reason. There is no rationale for 10-year-olds becoming adept at "computational thinking" (a buzzword promoted by the computer **industry**) when they cannot spell well.

This is just another ploy to sell machines to cash-strapped school districts. Nobody really cares about the kids. If they did, they'd emphasize the arts and music more.

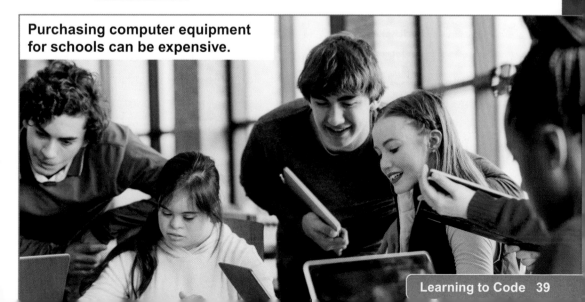

Purchasing computer equipment for schools can be expensive.

❷ PRO: Kids Can Code, No Problem

by Becky Button, 7th-Grade Student

Coding should become a core component of the elementary school curriculum.

Understanding computer **code** is an important part of what makes us literate in today's technology. **Coding involves** dividing up a task into its most basic pieces and then putting them together in a logical order. This **analytical** thinking **process** has lots of real-world applications.

I took my first class in the fourth grade, and I wish I had started sooner. I started out with a project on Boolean logic and truth tables. Next, I got interested in physical computing and started experimenting with microcontrollers (small computers). I learned about simple electrical circuits and then progressed to making robots.

My younger brother, who is in the third grade, already **codes**. He can do amazing things with **code**, like make his robot do tasks and create his own video games. For a recent social studies project, he used Scratch, a programming language, to make an animated video of the life of George Washington. He will be ahead of me by the time he is my age.

Elementary students can do this. There are already **coding** clubs for kids around this country and around the world. I am a member of one called CoderDojo, a free service that teaches kids ages 7 to 17 to learn to **code**, share ideas, and learn from each other.

Code is everywhere now. It's in your phone, it's in your kitchen appliances, it's in your car, it's in the cards we carry in our wallets, and it's how we communicate. Learning to code needs to be in the schools. If kids learn to **code**, they will understand the language that is shaping their future.

Technology CONTENT CONNECTION

Is learning to code like learning a foreign language?

Recently, some states have proposed laws that would allow students to meet their foreign language requirements by taking coding or computer programming classes. Many supporters believe that learning the language of computers is like learning a foreign language. However, many people and organizations argue that coding classes should be offered in addition to foreign language classes. Here are three reasons why:

- Foreign language classes are important, since students learn more than just a language—they learn about different cultures and countries, too.

- Learning to code and learning a foreign language are very different. For example, there are only about 100 words in most coding languages, but there can be over 10,000 words in some foreign languages.

- There's more to coding than learning the language. Coders need to learn all about computer science, which includes important math and science concepts.

TAKE A STAND

Should schools allow students to take coding instead of a foreign language?

Debate

ARE YOU WATCHING YOUR WATER USE?

Water is an important resource. But someday there may not be enough of it to go around. Less than one percent of Earth's water is available for human use. And as the population grows, the demand for water does, too.

Part of the problem is record low rainfall. In the southwestern United States, the situation is severe. Lakes are running dry and wildfires are springing up. Some cities have made wasting water against the law.

As dry areas wait for rain, people must save water. It's not hard. Studies show that small changes have big effects. For example, turning off the tap while brushing your teeth can save up to eight gallons of water a day.

How can you watch your water use?

With little or no rainfall, many parts of the country are experiencing a drought. What can communities do to prepare for drought?

All Dried Up

In 2014, **drought** impacted nearly 25% of the United States and 74.2 million Americans.

(Source: US Drought Portal, 2014)

Running on Empty

In 2014, over 80% of California experienced "extreme or exceptional" **drought** conditions.

(Source: US Drought Monitor, 2014)

According to researchers, the **drought** cost California $2.2 billion in 2014.

(Source: UC Davis Center for Watershed Sciences, 2014)

Stopping Water Waste

If you can keep your shower to under five minutes, you can save up to 1,000 gallons of water a month.

Turning off the water while you wash your hair can save up to 150 gallons of water a month.

(Source: Water—Use It Wisely Campaign, 2014)

Fines for Water Wasters

by Stephanie Kraus from *TIME For Kids*

Lakes have run dry, lawns have turned brown, and farmers have left land unplanted. The problems are a result of an extreme **drought** that has taken over nearly 80 percent of California. It is the state's worst **drought** in nearly 40 years. The conditions have led to wildfires and damage to animals' habitats. But too many residents are still not taking their state's **drought** seriously.

It is the state's worst drought in nearly 40 years.

Water regulators recently decided to fine California residents up to $500 a day if they are seen wasting water. The fines will apply only to wasteful outdoor water use, such as washing a vehicle with excess water or hosing down sidewalks and driveways.

"Outdoor water waste is unacceptable in a time of **drought**," Felicia Marcus told *TIME*. She heads the State Water Resources Control Board. "We don't know when it's going to rain again . . . this is a dramatic action, but these are dramatic times."

Three Years and Counting

California has had a **drought** for three years. In 2014, Governor Jerry Brown declared a state of emergency. Residents were told that if it didn't rain this winter, conditions in the state could get worse. Some farmers could see their wells run dry next year and communities could run out of drinking water. Yet too many California residents are not heeding the warnings. Five months later, water **consumption** in the state actually rose by one percent, according to a report from the board.

The board estimates that the new rules about water usage could save enough water to supply more than 3.5 million people for a year. Cities are free to decide how they will fine residents. Repeat violators could face the full $500-a-day fine. Others might receive warnings or smaller fines. The regulations went into effect in early August.

Marcus says the rules will send a message about how serious the situation is. "We were hoping for more voluntary **conservation**," she says. "We hope this will get people's attention."

The Problem Spreads

California is not the only state affected by the **drought**. States in the southwestern part of the United States are seeing problems too. Lake

Drought Damage

January 2013

January 2014

The damage of California's drought can be seen in these two satellite photos taken a year apart. In 2013, mountain snow, which makes up a third of California's drinking water, covers most of the land east of the Sierra Nevada. The land to the west of the Sierra Nevada is green and covered in plants. In 2014, after the worst of the drought, most of the snow and plants are gone.

Source: NASA Earth Observatory, 2014

Mead in Las Vegas, Nevada, has reached its lowest level since the 1930s. When the lake is full, it is about 1,296 feet above sea level. In 2014, the lake was about 1,082 feet above sea level, and the reservoir was about 39 percent full, according to Rose Davis. She is a spokeswoman for the US Bureau of Reclamation, a water-management agency, in Boulder City, Nevada.

"We projected this was coming," says Davis. "We are basically where we expected to be, given the dry winters in 2012 and 2013."

Las Vegas depends on Lake Mead for drinking water for its 2 million residents and 40 million tourists each year. If the lake drops seven feet more, Nevada and Arizona could face cuts in their water delivery. But Davis does not expect that to happen. The bureau predicts there will be a small increase in the water level by January 2015.

California Drought

In 2012, nearly 20 percent of California experienced severe to extreme drought. By 2014, 94 percent of California experienced severe to extreme drought.

| 2012 | 2013 | 2014 |

Abnormally Dry
Moderate Drought
Severe Drought
Extreme Drought
Exceptional Drought

Source: US Drought Monitor, 2014

A Dwindling River

As water demands rise, the Colorado River is running dry.

by Judith Jango-Cohen from *Super Science*

1 About 100 years ago, the Colorado River raged southward toward the Gulf of California. Where the two bodies of water met, great walls of water sprayed high into the sky. This amazing water show no longer happens. These days, the Colorado River often dries up before it even reaches the gulf.

> **As the world's population expands, the demand for water is rising.**

Like many of the world's sources of fresh water, the Colorado River is shrinking. People are draining away huge amounts of this water for personal use, such as drinking and bathing. Water is also used to grow crops and raise livestock, and in industrial processes. For instance, fresh water is used to manufacture goods like T-shirts and computers.

As the world's population expands, the demand for water is rising. Freshwater sources are now being drained more quickly than natural processes like rain can refill them. As a result, many parts of the world are facing water shortages. "Ensuring that everyone has enough fresh water will be one of the major **issues** facing us this century," says scientist Eleanor Sterling. She was in charge of the exhibition *Water: H2O = Life* at the American

Museum of Natural History in New York City, which highlighted water's many forms and uses.

Water Pressure

Roughly 70 percent of Earth's surface is covered in water. So how can there be a water shortage? Most of the water on Earth is salty. Less than three percent of it is fresh water, and only a tiny fraction of that is available for use.

In addition, freshwater sources are not spread evenly around the planet. Water shortages are greatest in arid **regions** like southern Africa and the southwestern United States. To make matters worse, the human populations in many of these **regions** are increasing.

Phoenix, Arizona, is one of these **regions**. The city and surrounding areas are home to roughly 3 million people. Thousands of people move there each year. Yet the city— located in the middle of the

Sonoran Desert—receives less than 25 centimeters (10 inches) of rain a year. That's only one-third of the national average.

Watering the Desert

How do people survive in the dry Southwest? Groundwater provides one source of fresh water. But there is not enough groundwater to meet the area's needs. The bulk of the water is taken from the Colorado River.

This 2,334-kilometer (1,450-mile)-long river supplies water to several big cities, including Las Vegas and San Diego. In all, it delivers fresh water to about 30 million people. The river also **irrigates** 14,973 square kilometers (3.7 million acres) of farmland.

❷ Southwest Distress

The demand for water is taking a toll on the river. Except in heavy flood years, dams and canals capture every drop of the Colorado River for use. As the **region's** population grows, the river is becoming unable to meet the demand for water.

Overuse of the Colorado River is threatening the water supply for homes, as well as for ranchers and farmers. But the drying river has also put wild plants and animals at risk. The Colorado River Delta was once brimming with wildlife. But little water reaches the delta now. As a result, many plants, bobcats, beavers, deer, shrimp, and several species of fish have lost a home.

The Hoover Dam directs water from the Colorado River to the Lake Mead reservoir.

Water Solutions

"To tackle the problem of water shortages, the focus should be on **conservation**—how to live with less of it," says Dr. Sterling.

Researchers are trying to help **reduce** water use by coming up with new ways to **irrigate** crops. "In the Southwest, large amounts of water [used to water crops] are lost to evaporation," says Dr. Sterling. So scientists are developing new **irrigation** methods that deliver water directly to plants' roots. This means less water would be lost to evaporation.

Personal Decisions

Dr. Sterling says that individuals also can make a difference when it comes to saving water. For instance,

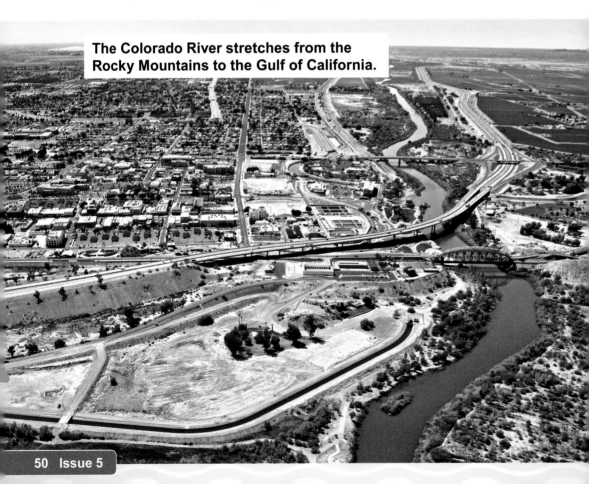

The Colorado River stretches from the Rocky Mountains to the Gulf of California.

instead of dumping leftover drinking water down the drain, use it to water plants. Another water-saving tip: don't leave the water running when you are brushing your teeth or washing dishes, says Dr. Sterling.

Other ways to **conserve** water are more surprising.

Water is used to manufacture computer chips in cell phones, cameras, laptops, and toys. So Dr. Sterling **recommends** purchasing no more of these items than you need. In addition to saving money, you'll be helping to protect the planet's water supply.

Soil, Sun, and Lots of Water

One of California's most important businesses is agriculture, or farming. The drought is having a big impact on farms. In 2014, nearly 99 percent of California farms experienced severe drought or worse.

California produces nearly half of the fruits and vegetables grown in the United States. The geography and climate of the Golden State provide a perfect farming environment. Crops like avocados and lemons are able to grow year-round. But aside from land and sunshine, farms need water . . . and lots of it. Farms use about 80 percent of California's water. And less water means fewer crops. With the state asking people to cut back on water use, should the same be asked of farmers?

TAKE A STAND

Should farms face the same water restrictions as citizens?

Debate

Is it ever okay to trick someone?

Folktales are stories that were told centuries ago, before being passed down from generation to generation. They can be serious and teach us a lesson, or funny and make us laugh. Trickster tales are one specific type of folktale. Tricksters may appear to be clumsy or weak, but they're always clever. Trickster tales often share a similar hero, but every culture adds its own twist to the story. The characters and lessons in folktales can teach us a lot about how we and other people live.

Pedro's Holey Sombrero

by Barbara Winther

CHARACTERS

STOREKEEPER

RICH MAN

WATCHMAKER

PEDRO

---

① TIME: *Morning.*

SETTING: *City street in Latin America. Left center, angled, is small table, two* **similar** *jackets spread out on it; right center, angled opposite way, is small table, two watches on it. Sign on easel in front of right curtain reads:* MORNING IN THE CITY.

AT RISE: STOREKEEPER, *arms crossed, stands upstage of left table.* WATCHMAKER *stands upstage of right table.* RICH MAN *enters left and crosses to* STOREKEEPER. PEDRO *enters right and crosses to* STOREKEEPER, *careful to stay clear of* RICH MAN, *but paying close attention to what he says and does.*

STOREKEEPER *(To* RICH MAN*)*: *Buenos dias, señor.* I have here two wonderful jackets for sale—fine material, latest style.

RICH MAN *(Examining jackets)*: Hm-m-m, these are nice jackets. I would look quite handsome wearing either one.

STOREKEEPER: I'm sure you would.

RICH MAN: How much are you asking for them?

STOREKEEPER: Only two hundred *pesos* each.

RICH MAN *(Disgusted)*: Two hundred *pesos*? That's way too much.

STOREKEEPER (*Spreading hands*)**:** It is a **bargain**. These are the best jackets on the market. (*Sighs*) Oh, well, if you buy both, you could have them for one hundred and ninety *pesos* each.

RICH MAN: That's still too much.

STOREKEEPER: Would you have me lose money on these jackets? Come on, *señor*. I am a poor man, and you are a rich man. The price is fair. You can **afford** both jackets.

RICH MAN: Of course I can **afford** them, but I'm only interested in the best **bargains**, and yours aren't good enough. (*STOREKEEPER shrugs, as does PEDRO.*) *Adiós*, Storekeeper. I shall visit the watchmaker instead. (*Crosses to WATCHMAKER, followed by PEDRO, still careful to stay out of RICH MAN's way. STOREKEEPER frowns and crosses arms.*)

WATCHMAKER (*To RICH MAN*)**:** *Buenos días, señor.*

I have here two excellent watches. Not only do they keep perfect time, but they are equally stylish.

RICH MAN (*Examining watches*)**:** Hm-m-m, nice watches. Either one would look fine on my wrist.

WATCHMAKER: I'm sure that's true.

RICH MAN: How much are you asking?

WATCHMAKER: Only four hundred *pesos* each.

RICH MAN (*Disgusted*)**:** Four hundred *pesos*? That's way too much.

WATCHMAKER (*Shaking head*)**:** No, it isn't. It's a **bargain**. These are quality watches. (*Sighs*) Oh, well, if you bought both I could give them to you for three hundred and fifty *pesos* each.

RICH MAN: That's still too much.

WATCHMAKER: It's a fair price. Would you have me lose money on these watches?

Señor, I'm a poor man; I have to make *some* **profit**. Surely you, a rich man, can **afford** to buy both watches.

RICH MAN: Of course I can **afford** them, but I'm only interested in the best **bargains**, and yours aren't good enough. *(Sets watches back on table) Adiós.* I'm going home to count my money. *(Starts right.* WATCHMAKER *shrugs as does* PEDRO. *Then* WATCHMAKER *crosses arms, sighs.* PEDRO *removes* sombrero *and hurries over and taps shoulder of* RICH MAN.*)*

PEDRO: *Señor*, excuse me.

RICH MAN *(Looking at him disdainfully):* You are Pedro, the peasant who used to work for me. *(Angrily)* What do you want now? I have no job for you.

PEDRO: I beg of you, *señor*, let me have a small **loan**. Lately, my luck has been bad. If you lend me fifty *pesos*, I will pay you back next week with good interest.

RICH MAN: I won't lend you even one *peso*.

PEDRO: Why not?

RICH MAN: In the first place, I don't like people with holes in their *sombreros. (Gestures*

distastefully at PEDRO's *hat*. PEDRO *frowns*.) In the second place, you don't have anything to offer me, so why should I help you? *Adíos. (Exits right, haughtily.* STOREKEEPER *and* WATCHMAKER *meet center, shaking heads, looking after* RICH MAN. PEDRO, *studying his hat, crosses to stand between them.)*

STOREKEEPER: That rich man is obnoxious.

WATCHMAKER (*Nodding*): He's always trying to get the best at the expense of others. He only cares about himself.

PEDRO (*Smiling at hat*): I know how we can get the best of him.

STOREKEEPER AND WATCHMAKER (*In unison*)**:** How?

PEDRO (*Putting on hat*): Listen, *mis amigos*. I have a plan to **outwit** the rich man, but I'll need your help. Agreed? *(Extends hand, palm up.* STOREKEEPER *and* WATCHMAKER *each slap a hand on his.)*

STOREKEEPER AND WATCHMAKER (*In unison*)**:** Agreed.

❷ *(Blackout.* **PEDRO** *exits left;* **STOREKEEPER** *and* **WATCHMAKER** *return to stand behind tables; new sign on easel reads: THE NEXT MORNING. Lights up.)*

RICH MAN (*Sauntering on right, counting money*): Ah, I made a good **profit** selling my sugar cane. *(Folds up money and puts it in pocket.* PEDRO *enters left and crosses to* STOREKEEPER.)*

PEDRO (*Picking up jacket*): How much is this fine jacket?

STOREKEEPER: Only two hundred *pesos*.

PEDRO: That's a **bargain**. I'll take it. Charge it to my *sombrero. (Slips on jacket)*

STOREKEEPER: *Sí*. The jacket is charged to your *sombrero*.

PEDRO: *Gracias. (*RICH MAN *is amazed, blinks,*

mouth open. PEDRO *crosses to* WATCHMAKER, *and picks up watch.)* How much is this fine watch?

WATCHMAKER: Only four hundred *pesos*.

PEDRO: That's a **bargain**. I'll take it. Charge it to my *sombrero. (Slips on watch)*

WATCHMAKER: *Sí.* The watch is charged to your *sombrero.*

PEDRO: *Gracias. (RICH MAN is even more amazed. PEDRO starts to pass him to exit right.)*

RICH MAN: Wait a minute. Wait a minute.

PEDRO *(Haughtily)*: What do you want?

RICH MAN: Yesterday you said you were down on your luck. You asked me for a **loan**. Today you are buying a jacket and a watch.

PEDRO: *Sí.*

RICH MAN: How can you do that?

PEDRO: I have discovered that my holey *sombrero* is far

more **valuable** than I **realized**. It is magical. I can go to any merchant and say, "Charge it to my *sombrero*," and the merchandise is mine.

RICH MAN: Amazing! What a **valuable** hat! You must sell it to me.

PEDRO *(Indignantly)*: Sell it to you! I should say not. Yesterday you wouldn't even lend me a *peso*.

RICH MAN: Forgive me. I must have been out of my mind. Look, I'll give you two hundred *pesos* for your *sombrero*.

PEDRO: No!

RICH MAN: Four hundred *pesos*.

PEDRO *(Louder)*: No!

RICH MAN *(Pulling out money)*: Six hundred.

PEDRO *(Looking at money)*: Well, I don't know.

RICH MAN: Eight hundred. My last offer. Take it or leave it.

PEDRO: I'll take it. You drive a hard **bargain**.

(*Hands him* sombrero, *takes money, exits right.* RICH MAN *gleefully rushes over to* WATCHMAKER.)

RICH MAN: I'll buy this watch. (*Picks it up*) Charge it to my *sombrero*.

WATCHMAKER: I can't do that.

RICH MAN: Of course you can. (*Runs to* STOREKEEPER *and picks up jacket*) Charge this to my *sombrero*, too.

STOREKEEPER: I can't do that.

RICH MAN: Of course you can, of course you can.

WATCHMAKER AND STOREKEEPER (*In unison*): No, we can't.

RICH MAN (*Sputtering to both*): But, but, you let Pedro charge a jacket and a watch to his *sombrero*. This is the same hat. Why can't I use it the same way?

WATCHMAKER: Because when Pedro owned that *sombrero*, it was the best he had. It was **valuable**.

STOREKEEPER: Whereas to a rich man, it is only a tattered hat, full of holes, and **worth** nothing. *(RICH MAN snarls and hurls hat to ground.)*

RICH MAN: I've been **tricked**. *(Runs off left, shaking fist)*

WATCHMAKER AND STOREKEEPER *(Shouting after him in unison)*: Adiós, señor. *(Burst into laughter.*

PEDRO *reenters, laughs, and counts money.)*

PEDRO *(To* WATCHMAKER*):* And here are four hundred *pesos* for my watch. *(Hands him money. To* STOREKEEPER*)* And here are two hundred *pesos* for my jacket. *(Hands him money. Pockets rest of money.)* And two hundred *pesos* for the **loan** of my holey *sombrero*. *(Puts hat on head. All cheer. Blackout. Curtain)*

THE END

Meet the Author

BARBARA WINTHER

Education: As an undergraduate, Winther majored in English and minored in art at the University of California, Los Angeles (UCLA). She later continued her education by doing post-graduate work at the University of California, Santa Barbara (UCSB).

Works: Winther is the author of many folklore and drama collections for children. She also writes about travel, history, and art.

Bio: In addition to writing, Winther has taught elementary school, run and operated a trading company specializing in Native American art, and been elected to the prestigious Society of Woman Geographers.

Little Red Riding Hood and the Wolf

by Roald Dahl

As soon as Wolf began to feel

That he would like a decent meal,

He went and knocked on Grandma's door.

When Grandma opened it, she saw

The sharp white teeth, the horrid grin,

And Wolfie said, "May I come in?"

Poor Grandmamma was terrified,

"He's going to eat me up!" she cried.

And she was absolutely right.

He ate her up in one big bite.

But Grandmamma was small and tough,

And Wolfie wailed, "That's not enough!

"I haven't yet begun to feel

"That I have had a decent meal!"

He ran around the kitchen yelping,

"I've *got* to have another helping!"

Then added with a frightful leer,

"I'm therefore going to wait right here

"Till Little Miss Red Riding Hood

"Comes home from walking in the wood."

He quickly put on Grandma's clothes,
(Of course he hadn't eaten those).
He dressed himself in coat and hat.
He put on shoes and after that
He even brushed and curled his hair,
Then sat himself in Grandma's chair.
In came the little girl in red.
She stopped. She stared. And then she said,

"*What great big ears you have, Grandma.*"
"*All the better to hear you with,*" the Wolf replied.
"*What great big eyes you have, Grandma.*"
   said Little Red Riding Hood.
"*All the better to see you with,*" the Wolf replied.

He sat there watching her and smiled.
He thought, I'm going to eat this child.
Compared with her old Grandmamma
She's going to taste like caviar.

Then Little Red Riding Hood said, "*But Grandma,
what a lovely great big furry coat you have on.*"

"That's wrong!" cried Wolf. "Have you forgot
"To tell me what BIG TEETH I've got?
"Ah well, no matter what you say,
"I'm going to eat you anyway."

The small girl smiles. One eyelid flickers.

She whips a pistol from her knickers.

She aims it at the creature's head

And *bang bang bang*, she shoots him dead.

A few weeks later, in the wood,

I came across Miss Riding Hood.

But what a change! No cloak of red,

No silly hood upon her head.

She said, "Hello, and do please note

"My lovely furry WOLFSKIN COAT."

Meet the Author

ROALD DAHL

Born: September 13, 1916, in Llandaff, South Wales

Died: November 23, 1990, in Oxford, England

Bio: Roald Dahl was born in Wales and raised in England. During World War II, he fought as a fighter pilot with England's Royal Air Force. After his plane crashed over Libya, a head injury prevented him from returning to combat. Soon after, Dahl moved to Washington, DC, to work for the war effort and write. Dahl started by writing and publishing stories for adults. It wasn't until he moved back to England with his own family that he tried writing for children. Dahl's children's stories became international sensations. Today, many are considered classics.

Works: Dahl's most famous books include *James and the Giant Peach*, *Matilda*, *The BFG*, and *Charlie and the Chocolate Factory*. Many of these books have been made into movies. Dahl also wrote screenplays for television shows and movies, including the James Bond film *You Only Live Twice*.

Use the academic language frames in this handbook as a reference during academic discussions.

The **heading** states the overall type of discussion or interaction.

Look for the **"If" statement** that most closely describes the specific type of interaction.

Look for examples of completed frames in **speech bubbles**.

ACADEMIC LANGUAGE HANDBOOK

Facilitating Discussion
Collaborate to have a discussion in a small group.

If you want to ask a group member about a word . . .
* So _____, are you familiar with the word _____?

If you want to share word knowledge with the group . . .
* I've never seen or heard the word _____.
* I recognize the word _____ but need to learn how to use it.
* I can use _____ in a sentence. For example, _____.
* I know that the word _____ means _____.

If you want to share word knowledge with the class . . .
* We don't know what _____ means yet.
* We think _____ means _____.
* Our example is similar to _____'s group.

If you want to select a classmate to share ideas . . .
* I pick _____.
* I select _____.
* I choose _____.
* I nominate _____.

If you want to share an idea . . .
* Something interesting I learned is that _____.
* I also learned that _____.
* One new fact I learned is that _____.
* Another interesting fact I learned is that _____.
* One piece of data that caught my attention is that _____.
* I didn't know that _____.

If you want to ask a classmate if you can share ideas with him or her . . .
* May I (share/discuss) ideas with you?

If you agree to share ideas with a classmate . . .
* Yes, (of course/absolutely/certainly).

Language Tip
Follow "For example, . . ." with a sentence that shows you are familiar with the word.
You could say, "I can use symptom in a sentence. For example, one symptom of a cold is a sore throat."

Another interesting fact I learned is that 19% of sports injuries for 8–11-year-olds are concussions.

Reporting Ideas
Share a partner or group's ideas during a class discussion.

If you are reporting a classmate's idea . . .
* _____'s idea was that _____.
* _____ (shared/stated) that _____.
* _____ pointed out that _____.

If you are choosing precise words . . .
* We thought of the precise word _____.
* We came up with the precise word _____.
* We selected the precise word _____.
* One (topic/high-utility) word we plan to use is _____.
* One (topic/high-utility) word we (located/identified) is _____.

If you are reporting responses . . .
* We thought of _____.
* We came up with _____.
* We chose _____.
* We selected _____.
* We decided upon _____.
* We agreed upon _____.

Elaborating
Provide more information and details to support a claim.

If you want to give an example . . .
* For (example/instance), _____.
* One example is _____.

If you want to share a personal experience . . .
* I know this because _____.
* The reason I know this is _____.
* I have found that _____.

We thought of the precise word "foolish."

Language Tip
"Instance" is a noun that is another way of saying "example."

Read the **Language Tips** to help you understand challenging language and how to complete frames with correct grammar.

Choose a **frame** to structure what you say. A **blank line** means that you need to complete the sentence. **Words in parentheses** mean you have a choice of using one of the words or phrases listed.

Requesting Assistance

Ask the teacher or a classmate for help.

you don't understand what the speaker said . . .

I couldn't hear you. Could you repeat that?

I didn't hear you. Please repeat your (idea/response).

you don't understand what the speaker meant . . .

I don't quite understand. Could you give me an example?

I am somewhat confused. Could you explain that again?

I am not sure I get your point. Could you explain what you mean by _____?

Asking for Clarification

Ask for more information.

you have a question . . .

I have a question about _____.

One question I have is _____?

you need information repeated . . .

Will you explain _____ again?

Will you explain the directions for this assignment again?

you need more explanation . . .

What do you mean by _____?

I don't quite understand your (question/suggestion).

What exactly do you mean by _____?

Could you explain what you mean by _____?

What exactly do you mean by "the topic sentence"?

Listening Actively

Show that you are an active listener.

you want to ask your partner about an idea . . .

What (ideas/example) did you (add/choose)?

What (ideas/example) did you (record/select)?

you want to share the idea you added . . .

I (added/chose/recorded/selected) _____.

Facilitating Discussion

Collaborate to have a discussion in a small group.

If you want to ask a group member about a word . . .
- So _____, are you familiar with the word _____?

If you want to share word knowledge with the group . . .
- I've never seen or heard the word _____.
- I recognize the word _____ but need to learn how to use it.
- I can use _____ in a sentence. For example, _____.
- I know that the word _____ means _____.

If you want to share word knowledge with the class . . .
- We don't know what _____ means yet.
- We think _____ means _____.
- Our example is similar to _____'s group.

If you want to select a classmate to share ideas . . .
- I pick _____.
- I choose _____.
- I select _____.
- I nominate _____.

If you want to share an idea . . .
- Something interesting I learned is that _____.
- I also learned that _____.
- One new fact I learned is that _____.
- Another interesting fact I learned is that _____.
- One piece of data that caught my attention is that _____.
- I didn't know that _____.

If you want to ask a classmate if you can share ideas with him or her . . .
- May I (share/discuss) ideas with you?

If you agree to share ideas with a classmate . . .
- Yes, (of course/absolutely/certainly).

Language Tip

Follow "For example, . . ." with a sentence that shows you are familiar with the word.

You could say, "I can use **symptom** in a sentence. For example, one symptom of a cold is a sore throat."

Another interesting fact I learned is that 19% of sports injuries for 8–11-year-olds are concussions.

Reporting Ideas

Share a partner or group's ideas during a class discussion.

If you are reporting a classmate's idea . . .

- _____'s idea was that _____.
- _____ (shared/stated) that _____.
- _____ pointed out that _____.

If you are choosing precise words . . .

- We thought of the precise word _____.
- We came up with the precise word _____.
- We selected the precise word _____.
- One (topic/high-utility) word we plan to use is _____.
- One (topic/high-utility) word we (located/identified) is _____.

> We thought of the precise word "foolish."

If you are reporting responses . . .

- We thought of _____.
- We came up with _____.
- We chose _____.
- We selected _____.
- We decided upon _____.
- We agreed upon _____.

Elaborating

Provide more information and details to support a claim.

If you want to give an example . . .

- For (example/instance), _____.
- One example is _____.

If you want to share a personal experience . . .

- I know this because _____.
- The reason I know this is _____.
- I have found that _____.

Language Tip

"Instance" is a noun that is another way of saying "example."

ACADEMIC LANGUAGE HANDBOOK

Restating Ideas

Listen carefully and repeat classmates' ideas in your own words.

If you want to restate someone else's idea . . .
- So you think that _____.
- So what you're saying is _____.
- In other words, what you mean is _____.
- So what you're suggesting is that _____.

> So what you're saying is that you think robots would make good teachers?

If someone restates your idea correctly . . .
- Yes, that's (right/correct).

If someone restates your idea incorrectly . . .
- No, not (really/exactly). What I meant was _____.

Agreeing & Disagreeing

Politely tell others if you agree or disagree with their ideas.

Language Tip
When you "don't quite" agree with something, you might only agree with part of what was said.

If you agree with an idea . . .
- I agree with _____'s (idea/opinion).

If you disagree with an idea . . .
- I disagree with _____'s idea.
- I don't quite agree with _____'s idea.
- I don't quite agree with _____'s opinion.

Comparing Ideas

Discuss how your ideas are similar to or different from others' ideas.

> My idea is different from Jessica's. I think schools should offer coding classes.

If your idea is similar . . .
- My idea is similar to _____'s.

If your idea is different . . .
- My idea is different from _____'s.

Negotiating With Others

Persuade others and support your opinions.

If you want to provide a counterargument . . .
- I agree with _____, but _____?
- That's a good point, but _____?

Collaborating With Others

Discuss responses with a partner or group members.

If you want to ask a classmate to respond . . .

- What should we write?
- What do you think (fits well/makes sense/is a strong choice)?

If you want to share your response with a classmate . . .

- We could (put/choose/select) _____.
- I think _____ (fits well/makes sense/is a strong choice).

If you want to agree on an idea . . .

- That would work.
- That works well.
- Okay. Let's write _____.

Offering Feedback

Share feedback and suggestions about a peer's work.

If you want to give positive feedback . . .

- I liked how you (used/included) _____.
- You did a great job on _____.
- I appreciate how you (used/included) _____.
- I appreciated the specific example of _____ that you included.
- Your concrete detail(s) about _____ strengthened your response.
- Your use of the word _____ was skillful.

If you want to offer a suggestion . . .

- Your (writing/speech) will be stronger if you _____.
- You could improve your (writing/speech) if you _____.
- One suggestion I have to improve your (writing/speech) is _____.
- I think you misspelled the word _____.
- The word _____ is actually spelled _____.
- Adding _____ would make your response (clearer/stronger).

> **Language Tip**
>
> Give examples of how to complete the frames to give positive feedback.
>
> For example, "You did a great job on including transitions to connect your ideas."

> You could improve your opinion essay if you include relevant text evidence to support your claim.

Predicting

Share what you think a text will be about.

If you want share what you think a text will be about . . .

- I predict the text will focus on _____.
- I predict the author will primarily address _____.

Summarizing

State the key ideas and details of a text.

If you want to ask what the key idea and details are. . .

- What is the key idea of this text?
- What is the author's main idea?
- What is this text (primarily/mainly) about?
- What does this text focus on?
- What are the most important details in this text?
- What are the key details in this text?
- What are the most essential details in the text?

> The author's main idea is that people who waste water should be fined.

If you want to state the key idea . . .

- The key idea of this text is _____.
- The author's main idea is _____.
- The text is (primarily/mainly) about _____.
- This text focuses on _____.

If you want to describe key details . . .

- (One/Another) important detail in this text is _____.
- (One/Another) key detail in this text is _____.
- (One/An additional) essential detail is _____.
- (One/An additional) significant detail is _____.
- Perhaps the most (important/significant/relevant) detail in this text is _____.

Language Tip

Choose a precise adjective that fits the detail you describe:

- An "essential" detail proves a point or supports a topic.

- A "significant" detail has an important influence or effect on the topic or issue.

- A "relevant" detail is related to your position.

Reacting to Text or Multimedia

Share your initial reactions, questions, or confusion about a text or multimedia.

If you want to share new ideas that you learned . . .

Something interesting I learned is _____.

One new fact I learned is _____.

After reading the text, one detail that caught my attention is _____.

I thought it was interesting that _____.

If you want to learn more about a topic . . .

I'm curious about _____.

I'd like to learn more about why _____.

I'd like to explore why _____.

The (video/audiobook/slideshow) made me interested in learning more about _____.

If you are confused . . .

I still don't (get/understand/comprehend) _____.

After (viewing/listening to) the multimedia, I still don't understand _____.

Language Tip

The expression "caught my attention" means "made me take notice."

> The video made me interested in learning more about other versions of the Little Red Riding Hood story.

Affirming & Clarifying Ideas

Acknowledge a classmate's idea, or ask for more information.

If you want to acknowledge others' ideas . . .

I see what you mean.

I hadn't thought of that.

I appreciate your story.

If you want to clarify others' ideas . . .

What do you mean by _____?

What exactly do you mean by _____?

Could you explain what you mean by _____?

Could you elaborate on _____?

One question I have is _____?

In other words, you think that _____?

> Could you elaborate on how you felt after your sister played a trick on you?

Vocabulary to Analyze Context

Use these terms to analyze and discuss the meaning of unfamiliar words.

analyze
verb to carefully examine something to understand it

analysis
noun a careful examination of something to understand it

context
noun the language surrounding a word or phrase that helps you understand it

prefix
noun a group of letters added to the beginning of a word to change its meaning
mis + understand = misunderstand

suffix
noun a letter or group of letters added to the end of a word that changes the part of speech
polite (adjective) + ness = politeness (noun)

root word
noun a word that is used as a base to create other words by adding a prefix or suffix, often coming from Greek or Latin
un + think + able = unthinkable

Common Prefixes & Suffixes

Learn these affixes to use as clues to the meanings of unfamiliar words.

Prefix	Meaning	Example Words
com–	together	*communicate, complicated*
dis–	not, opposite of	*discouraged, distastefully*
im–, in–	not	*inappropriate, indifference*
inter–	between	*interact, interaction*
mis–	bad, wrong	*mischief, mischievous*
non–, un–	not	*unstructured, unacceptable*
pre–	before	*preserve, prevent*
re–	again	*recycle, recover, reverse*
trans–	across	*transform, translate*

Suffix	Meaning	Example Words
–able, –ible *(adj)*	something that is possible	*unacceptable, accessible*
–ate *(verb)*	to make, cause, or act	*communicate, regulate*
–er, –or *(noun)*	someone or something who does	*communicator, generator*
–ial, –al *(adj)*	having characteristics of	*social, mechanical, original*
–ity *(noun)*	state of	*identity, ability*
–ive *(adj)*	having a particular quality	*effective*
–ment *(noun)*	the result	*environment, achievement*
–ous *(noun)*	having the qualities of	*mischievous*
–tion, –ion *(noun)*	the act or result of doing something	*preservation, communication*

Use the descriptions and transitions for the writing types in this handbook as a reference for your academic writing assignments.

Formal Summary

Academic Writing Type

A *formal summary* is a type of informative writing. It provides an overview of the topic and important details from an informational text. The writer credits the author, but writes original sentences using precise words. A summary does not include the writer's personal opinions.

A. The **topic sentence** includes the text type, title, author, and topic.

B. **Detail sentences** include the most important details from the text.

- **Transition words or phrases** help introduce and connect ideas.

C. The **concluding sentence** restates the author's conclusion in the writer's own words.

Topic Sentence
Important Detail 1
Important Detail 2
Important Detail 3
Concluding Sentence

Transitions

Use these transitions to introduce and connect ideas in a formal summary.

- In the article, _____.
- First, _____.
- The author also _____.

- In addition, _____.
- Furthermore, _____.

Opinion Paragraph

Academic Writing Type

*An **opinion paragraph** states a claim and supports it with logical reasons and relevant evidence from the texts.*

A. The **introductory sentence** clearly states the writer's claim about the issue.

B. **Detail sentences** support the claim with reasons and evidence from the text or the writer's experience.

- **Transition words or phrases** connect opinions, reasons, and evidence.

C. The **concluding sentence** restates the writer's claim about the issue.

Introductory Sentence
Reason 1
Evidence
Reason 2
Evidence
Concluding Sentence

Transitions

Use these transitions to connect opinions, reasons, and evidence.

- One reason _____.
- In my experience, _____.
- According to the article, _____.

- In fact, _____.
- For instance, _____.
- For these reasons, _____.

ACADEMIC WRITING HANDBOOK

Summary & Response

Academic Writing Type

*A **summary and response** provides an overview of the topic and important details from a text and then presents the writer's position on the issue.*

A. The **summary** includes a topic sentence, detail sentences, and a concluding sentence.

B. The **response** includes a transitional sentence that states the writer's claim, detail sentences that support the claim with reasons and evidence, and a concluding sentence.

Summary

Topic Sentence
Important Details
Concluding Sentence

Response

Transitional Sentence
Reasons & Evidence
Concluding Sentence

Transitions

Use these transitions to organize the details of your summary and response.

- In the article, _____.
- First, _____.
- In addition, _____.
- Furthermore, _____.

- The main reason I am (in favor of/ opposed to) _____ is _____.
- According to the text, _____.
- For this critical reason, _____.

Opinion Essay

Academic Writing Type

*An **opinion essay** states a claim and supports it with logical reasons and relevant evidence from the texts.*

A. The **introductory sentence** clearly states the writer's claim about the issue.

B. Each **supporting paragraph** includes:
  - A **topic sentence** that states what the paragraph will be about
  - **Detail sentences** that support the writer's claim with logical reasons and evidence from the text or the writer's experience
  - **Transition words or phrases** connect opinions, reasons, and evidence

C. The **concluding sentence** restates the writer's claim about the issue.

Introductory Sentence

Supporting Paragraph 1: Reason & Evidence

Supporting Paragraph 2: Reason & Evidence

Concluding Sentence

Transitions

Use these transitions to connect opinions, reasons, and evidence.

- One reason _____.
- The article states _____.
- Another key reason is _____.
- In fact, _____.
- According to the text, _____.
- For these reasons, _____.

Informative Text

Academic Writing Type

*An **informative text** examines a topic and conveys ideas and information.*

A. The **introductory sentence** introduces the topic and states the main idea.

B. Each **supporting paragraph** includes:

- A **topic sentence** that states what the paragraph will be about
- **Detail sentences** that develop the topic with facts, details, or quotations
- **Transition words or phrases** that introduce and connect ideas

C. The **concluding sentence** restates the topic and main idea.

Introductory Sentence

Supporting Paragraph 1: Facts, Details, or Quotations

Supporting Paragraph 2: Facts, Details, or Quotations

Concluding Sentence

Transitions

Use these transitions to introduce and connect ideas in your informative text.

- One clear benefit _____.
- For example, _____.
- However, _____.

- One reason _____.
- In contrast, _____.
- According to the text, _____.

Narrative

Academic Writing Type

*A **narrative** tells a story. It can be either fiction or nonfiction. A personal narrative tells a story from the writer's life and tells how his or her life changed as a result.*

A. The **introduction** identifies the characters, setting, and topic.

B. **Detail sentences** tell the most important events of the story.
  - **Transition words or phrases** show the order of events.
  - **Descriptive language** makes the story more vivid and interesting.

C. The **conclusion** explains the importance of the story.

Introduction

Important Event 1
Important Event 2
Important Event 3

Conclusion

Transitions

Use these transitions to help move the reader through the events of your narrative.

- During _____.
- So, _____.
- After that, _____.

- At that moment, _____.
- Clearly, _____.
- As a result, _____.

ACADEMIC GLOSSARY

A glossary is a useful tool found at the back of many books. It contains information about key words in the text. Review the sample glossary entry below.

This is an **entry word**— the word you look up. It is divided into syllables. Words in bold are Words to Know and words highlighted in yellow are Words to Go.

The **pronunciation** comes after the entry word. Letters and letter combinations stand for different sounds. The stressed syllable is marked in bold letters.

The **meaning** of the word follows the part of speech.

The **part of speech** follows the pronunciation.

A **number** appears at the beginning of each meaning if more than one meaning is given for the entry word.

The **Spanish cognate** is a word that looks or sounds the same in Spanish and has a similar meaning.

de•sign
(di-**zine**)

1. **verb** to draw a plan for something that will be made or built. *My classmate and I will carefully design our project for the science fair.*
Spanish cognate: *diseñar*

2. **noun** the way that something has been planned and made. *Whoever created the interior design for the new fitness center did a terrific job.*
Spanish cognate: *diseño*
Origin: Latin *designare*, meaning "to designate"

The **origin** of the word tells you the meaning of the word's Greek or Latin root.

The entry word is used in an **example sentence** that is in italics.

a·bil·i·ty
(uh-**bil**-i-tee)
noun a person's level of skill at doing something. *Marta has exceptional ability as a tennis player, and she wins almost every game.*
Origin: Latin *habilis,* meaning "able"
Spanish cognate: habilidad

ac·ces·si·ble
(ak-**sess**-uh-buhl)
adjective able to be approached, entered, or seen. *Books and other materials at the library are freely accessible to almost anyone who wants to use them.*
Origin: Latin *accedere,* meaning "to approach"
Spanish cognate: accesible

ac·com·plish
(uh-**kom**-plish)
verb to do something successfully. *Clearing snow from the driveway is a big job, but my sister and I can accomplish it easily.*
Origin: Latin *ad-,* meaning "to" + *complere,* meaning "to complete"

a·chieve
(uh-**cheev**)
verb to do something successfully; to reach a goal. *Nothing is impossible to achieve if you have faith in yourself.*

a·chieve·ment
(uh-**cheev**-muhnt)
noun a child's or student's progress in learning; something done successfully. *Getting great grades on a report card is a remarkable achievement.*

a·chiev·er
(uh-**cheev**-ur)
noun a person who reaches a goal or does something successfully. *If you want to be an achiever, you must be willing to work hard and not give up.*

af·ford
*(*uh-**ford***)*
verb to have enough money to buy something. *My neighbor paid me for helping him with his yard work, so I can easily afford the price of a movie ticket.*

an·a·lyt·ic·al
(an-uh-**lit**-uh-kuhl)
adjective thinking about things in a detailed way. *That is a complicated question, so we must take an analytical approach to answering it.*
Spanish cognate: analítico(a)

an·a·lyze
(**an**-uh-lize)
verb to think about something carefully to understand it. *We need to analyze the problem in depth before we can suggest a way to solve it.*
Spanish cognate: analizar

ap·pli·ca·tion
(ap-luh-**kay**-shuhn)
noun a way of using something. *That is an interesting theory, but what practical application does it have?*
Origin: Latin *applicare,* meaning "attach to, join, connect"
Spanish cognate: aplicación

ACADEMIC GLOSSARY

ap•pro•pri•ate
(uh-**proh**-pree-uht)
adjective correct or right for a situation or purpose. *It would be appropriate to send a get-well card to your sick cousin.*
Origin: Latin *ad-*, meaning "to" + *proprius,* meaning "own, proper"
Spanish cognate: apropiado(a)

ar•id
(**a**-rid)
adjective extremely dry. *Death Valley, which averages only a few inches of rain each year, is the most arid place in North America.*
Origin: Latin *arere*, meaning "be dry or parched"
Spanish cognate: árido(a)

as•sign•ment
(uh-**sine**-muhnt)
noun a piece of work or a job that a person is asked to do. *The spy accepted the dangerous assignment because she knew that she could do the job.*
Origin: Latin *assignare*, meaning "to sign"

bal•ance
(**bal**-uhnss)
noun a state in which opposite parts are equal or in the correct amounts. *Doctors must find a delicate balance between being professional and being compassionate.*
Origin: Latin *bilanx*, meaning "having two pans" (as in a scale)

bar•gain
(**bar**-guhn)
noun something you buy for a price that is lower than usual. *We found an amazing bargain on a chest of drawers at the thrift store.*

code
(**kode**)
1. *noun* the instructions of a computer program. *My brother is writing the code for a new app.*
Spanish cognate: código

2. *verb* to write the instructions of a computer program. *If you code this set of instructions differently, the program will run more smoothly.*
Origin: Latin *codex, codic*, meaning "book"

cod•ing
(**kod**-ing)
1. *noun* the process of writing the instructions of a computer program. *After we designed the program, all that was left was the coding.*
Spanish cognate: codificación

2. *verb* writing the instructions of a computer program. *I am coding this set of instructions now and should finish tomorrow.*

co•in•ci•dence
(koh-**in**-si-duhnss)
noun a situation in which two events happen at the same time by chance. *It was a lucky coincidence that our teacher canceled the math quiz because I forgot to study.*
Origin: Latin *co-*, meaning "together with" + *incidere*, meaning "fall upon or into"
Spanish cognate: coincidencia

col•li•sion
(kuh-**li**-shuhn)
noun a forceful crash, often at high speed. *The collision between the two trucks shut down the highway for hours.*
Origin: Latin *collidere*, meaning "strike together"
Spanish cognate: colisión

com•pli•cat•ed
(**kom**-pli-kay-tid)
adjective difficult to use or understand because of having many parts or details. *Your plan sounds very complicated; could you explain it again?*
Origin: Latin *com-*, meaning "together" + *plicare*, meaning "to fold"
Spanish cognate: complicado(a)

com•po•nent
(kuhm-**poh**-nuhnt)
noun a part of a machine or system. *Secrecy is an important component of our plans for Peter's surprise party.*
Origin: Latin *com-*, meaning "together" + *ponere*, meaning "put"
Spanish cognate: componente

con•di•tion
(kuhn-**dish**-uhn)
noun a medical problem, especially one that continues for some time. *Doctors finally were able to find a treatment for the patient's serious condition.*
Origin: Latin *con-*, meaning "with" + *dicere*, meaning "say"

con•ser•va•tion
(kon-sur-**vay**-shuhn)
noun the act of using as little of a resource as possible so that it is not wasted. *The goal of the new policy is the conservation of our state's forests.*
Spanish cognate: conservación

con•ser•va•tion•ist
(kon-sur-**vay**-shuhn-ist)
noun a person who tries to protect resources so that they are not wasted. *The conservationist became very upset when he saw how polluted the lake had become.*
Spanish cognate: conservacionista

con•serve
(kuhn-**surv**)
verb to use a resource carefully so that it is not wasted. *At our house, one way that we conserve energy is by using only as many lights as we absolutely need at any time.*
Origin: Latin *con-*, meaning "together" + *servare*, meaning "to keep"
Spanish cognate: conservar

con•sump•tion
(kuhn-**sump**-shuhn)
noun the amount of oil, electricity, or other resource that is used up. *Our utility bill went down when we cut back on our electricity consumption.*
Origin: Latin *con-*, meaning "altogether" + *sumere*, meaning "take up"
Spanish cognate: consumo

ACADEMIC GLOSSARY

de•cline
(di-**kline**)
verb to get worse, smaller, or fewer in number. *When this new smartphone becomes available, sales of the earlier version will decline dramatically.*
Origin: Latin *de-*, meaning "down" + *clinare*, meaning "to bend"

del•ta
(**del**-tuh)
noun a triangle-shaped piece of land where a river leaves mud, sand, or pebbles as it flows into the sea. *The place where the Nile River flows into the Mediterranean Sea is a very large delta.*
Spanish cognate: delta

de•sign
(di-**zine**)
1. *verb* to draw a plan for something that will be made or built. *My classmate and I will carefully design our project for the science fair.*
   Spanish cognate: diseñar
2. *noun* the way that something has been planned and made. *Whoever created the interior design for the new fitness center did a terrific job.*
   Spanish cognate: diseño
Origin: Latin *designare*, meaning "to designate"

de•tect
(di-**tekt**)
verb to notice, recognize, or discover something. *The police were unable to detect any lies in the witness's statement.*
Origin: Latin *de-*, meaning "opposite of" + *tegere*, meaning "to cover"

dis•cour•aged
(diss-**kur**-ijd)
verb made unlikely to happen because of a show of disapproval. *Students are strongly discouraged from bringing junk food to school.*

dis•pute
(diss-**pyoot**)
verb to disagree with or argue against someone or something. *You can't dispute the facts; the answer is clear.*
Origin: Latin *dis-*, meaning "apart" + *putare*, meaning "reckon"
Spanish cognate: disputar

dis•taste•ful•ly
(diss-**tayst**-fuhl-lee)
adverb done in a way that shows displeasure or a sense of being offended. *The child frowned and looked distastefully at the cabbage on his plate.*

drought
(**drout**)
noun a long period of dry weather. *Because of the severe drought this year, local farmers lost some of their crops.*

ef•fec•tive
(uh-**fek**-tiv)
adjective having the intended result. *This medicine should prove effective in making you feel better.*
Origin: Latin *efficere*, meaning "accomplish"
Spanish cognate: eficaz

en•croach•ment
(en-**croach**-muhnt)
noun an unwanted arrival or spread of something; an invasion. *When we noticed an encroachment of weeds, we cleaned out our vegetable garden in a hurry.*

ex•tent
(ek-**stent**)
noun the level or seriousness of something. *No one responded to the situation at first because no one realized the true extent of the problem.*
Origin: Latin *extendere*, meaning "stretch out"

fine
(**fine**)
1. *verb* to make someone pay money as a punishment. *The government can fine people who don't follow the law.*
2. *noun* an amount of money charged as a punishment. *When I parked in a no-parking zone, I needed to pay a $200 fine to the city.*
Origin: Latin *finis*, meaning "end"

gen•der
(**jen**-dur)
noun characteristics that society defines as male, female, both, or neither. *Differences in clothing and hairstyles often depend on a person's gender.*
Spanish cognate: género

haugh•ti•ly
(haw-**tuh**-lee)
adverb done in a way that shows feelings of superiority and contempt. *The conceited prince spoke haughtily to his servants and never even bothered to learn their names.*
Origin: Latin *altus*, meaning "high"

i•den•ti•fy
(eye-**den**-tuh-fye)
verb to recognize or tell what something is or who someone is. *I can correctly identify most of the kinds of butterflies that live in this area.*
Origin: Latin *idem*, meaning "same" + *facere*, meaning "make"
Spanish cognate: identificar

in•ap•pro•pri•ate
(in-uh-**proh**-pree-it)
adjective incorrect or wrong for a situation or purpose. *Laughing in a graveyard is inappropriate behavior.*
Origin: Latin *in-*, meaning "not" + *ad-*, meaning "to" + *proprius*, meaning "own, proper"
Spanish cognate: inapropiado(a)

in•dus•try
(**in**-duh-stree)
noun a group of businesses that make a certain thing or provide a certain service. *Jayden would love a career in the entertainment industry someday.*
Origin: Latin *industria*, meaning "diligence"
Spanish cognate: industria

in•jure
(**in**-jur)
verb to cause damage or harm to part of your body. *Falling on ice may not seem like a big deal, but it can seriously injure you.*

in•jured
(**in**-jurd)
adjective damaged or harmed. *The football player's badly injured knee caused him to miss the rest of the season.*

ACADEMIC GLOSSARY

in•ju•ry
(**in**-juh-ree)
noun damage or harm to part of your body. *Because of an old football injury, Dad sometimes suffers from pain in his shoulder.*
Origin: Latin *in-*, meaning "not" + *jus, jur-*, meaning "right"

in•ter•act
(in-tur-**akt**)
verb to talk, work, or play together. *In this dog obedience class, trainers will interact closely with their dogs.*
Origin: Latin *inter-*, meaning "between" + *agere*, meaning "to do"

in•ter•ac•tion
(in-tur-**ak**-shuhn)
noun activity between people or things. *In our reading group, we talk about stories and have a lot of face-to-face interaction.*
Spanish cognate: interacción

in•volve
(in-**volv**)
verb to include someone or something as a part of an activity or situation. *My activities tomorrow afternoon involve soccer practice and studying for a science test.*
Origin: Latin *in-*, meaning "into" + *volvere*, meaning "to roll"
Spanish cognate: involucrar

ir•ri•gate
(**ihr**-uh-gate)
verb to supply land or crops with water. *These farmers use canals to irrigate their land.*
Origin: Latin *in-*, meaning "into" + *rigare*, meaning "moisten, wet"
Spanish cognate: regar

ir•ri•ga•tion
(ihr-uh-**gay**-shuhn)
noun an artificial method of watering crops, such as through channels or pipes. *Are these ditches used for irrigation on this farm?*
Spanish cognate: irrigación

is•sue
(**ish**-oo)
noun a topic or problem. *People often argue over the issue of violence in video games.*
Origin: Latin *ex-*, meaning "out" + *ire*, meaning "go"

knick•ers
(**nik**-urz)
noun loose, short pants that end just below the knee. *This old photograph shows my great-grandfather as a boy, dressed in knickers and knee socks and holding a toy sailboat.*

leer
(**lihr**)
noun a sly or evil grin. *In the movie, the villain's leer let the audience know that he was up to no good.*

lim•it
(**lim**-it)
1. *verb* to stop something from going beyond a certain point. *Mom and Dad limit my use of the home computer to an hour a day.*
   Spanish cognate: limitar
2. *noun* the greatest amount or number allowed. *The speed limit along this road is 55 miles per hour.*
   Spanish cognate: límite
Origin: Latin *limit-*, meaning "boundary, frontier"

loan
(**lohn**)
noun money that one borrows or lends to someone. *My older sister has applied for a loan so that she can buy a car.*

man•u•fac•ture
(man-yuh-**fak**-chur)
verb to make something, often through the use of machines. *Two factories in my town manufacture furniture.*

me•chan•i•cal
(muh-**kan**-uh-kuhl)
adjective using power from a machine or engine. *Doing math with a mechanical calculator is usually faster than doing it in your head.*
Origin: Greek *mēkhanē*, meaning "contrivance"
Spanish cognate: mecánico(a)

mer•chan•dise
(**mur**-chuhn-disse)
noun goods that are bought or sold. *We were surprised at the many different kinds of merchandise for sale at the thrift store.*
Spanish cognate: mercancías

mis•chief
(**miss**-chif)
noun behavior that may cause trouble but no serious harm. *Dad warned us, "Be good, and stay out of mischief while I'm away!"*

mis•chie•vous
(**miss**-chuh-vuhss)
adjective behaving in a way that may cause trouble but no serious harm. *That mischievous child always seems to be misbehaving.*

oc•cur
(uh-**kur**)
verb to take place or happen. *Dust storms rarely occur around here, but they do happen sometimes.*
Origin: Latin *occurrere*, meaning "go to meet, present itself"
Spanish cognate: ocurrir

out•wit
(out-**wit**)
verb to fool or trick someone by being more clever. *In this story, will the wolf catch the rabbit, or will the rabbit outwit him and get away?*

ploy
(**ploi**)
noun a clever and sometimes unethical plan to benefit from a situation. *The child pretended to be sick so that he could stay home from school, but his mother discovered the clever ploy and sent him to school anyway.*

ACADEMIC GLOSSARY

pol·i·cy
(**pol**-uh-see)
noun a rule or certain way of doing something. *The school has a strict policy about using the computers in the library.*
Origin: Greek *polis*, meaning "city"
Spanish cognate: política

pre·vent
(pri-**vent**)
verb to stop something from happening. *Can a flu shot prevent me from getting sick this winter?*
Origin: Latin *prae*, meaning "before" + *venire*, meaning "come"
Spanish cognate: prevenir

pre·vi·ous·ly
(**pree**-vee-uhs-lee)
adverb in an earlier time; beforehand. *I know what I said previously, but now I've changed my mind.*
Origin: Latin *praevius*, meaning "going before"

proc·ess
(**pross**-ess)
noun the steps or actions used to produce something. *A person who wants to run for public office will find that it is a complex political process.*
Origin: Latin *processus*, meaning "progression, course"
Spanish cognate: proceso

prof·it
(**prof**-it)
noun money gained by selling things, after the costs have been paid. *Uncle Ray bought an old house, fixed it up, and sold it at a huge profit.*
Origin: Latin *profectus*, meaning "progress, profit"

pro·gram
(**proh**-gram)
verb to write a set of instructions for a computer. *I could design a great video game if only I knew how to program a computer.*
Origin: Greek *pro-*, meaning "before" + *graphein*, meaning "write"
Spanish cognate: programar

re·ac·tion
(ree-**ak**-shuhn)
noun something that someone feels or does in response to something. *Aunt Maria's reaction to our surprise was to gasp and then give us a big smile.*
Origin: Latin *re-*, meaning "back" + *agere*, meaning "do, act"
Spanish cognate: reacción

re·al·ize
(**ree**-uh-lize)
verb to come to understand something. *This isn't a joke; you don't realize how important this decision is to me.*

rec·om·mend
(rek-uh-**mend**)
verb to advise someone to do something. *Felipe and Jason highly recommend that we see this movie; they say that it is terrific.*
Origin: Latin *re-*, meaning "once more" + *commendare*, meaning "commit to one's care"
Spanish cognate: recomendar

re•cov•er
(ri-**kuhv**-ur)
verb to get better after an illness or injury. *I'm sorry that you're sick, but I hope that you'll recover quickly.*
Origin: Latin *recuperare*, meaning "get again"
Spanish cognate: recuperarse

re•cov•er•y
(ri-**kuhv**-uh-ree)
noun the act or process of getting better after an illness or injury. *I had a slow but full recovery from my broken leg.*
Spanish cognate: recuperación

re•duce
(ri-**dooss**)
verb to make something smaller in size or amount. *The company attempted to reduce its costs by letting go some of its employees.*
Origin: Latin *re-*, meaning "back, again" + *ducere*, meaning "bring, lead"
Spanish cognate: reducir

re•gion
(**ree**-juhn)
noun a large area of the country or world. *The western part of that country is a mountainous region.*
Origin: Latin *regio(n-)*, meaning "direction, district"
Spanish cognate: región

re•place
(ri-**playss**)
verb to take the place of or to substitute for someone or something. *The lightbulb in this lamp burned out, so I simply will replace it with a new bulb.*
Spanish cognate: reemplazar

res•i•dent
(**rez**-uh-duhnt)
noun someone who lives in a particular place. *Every resident of my apartment building enjoys working in our community garden.*
Origin: Latin *residere*, meaning "remain"
Spanish cognate: residente

re•spond
(ri-**spond**)
verb to say, write, or do something as a reaction or reply. *I was so surprised by the news that I didn't know how to respond.*
Origin: Latin *re-*, meaning "again" + *spondere*, meaning "to pledge"
Spanish cognate: responder

ro•bot
(**roh**-bot)
noun a machine that may look something like a human and that is programmed to do complex tasks. *Each robot in this factory has a specialized job.*
Spanish cognate: robot

ro•bot•ic
(roh-**bot**-ik)
adjective like a machine that may resemble a human and that is programmed to do complex tasks. *Robotic landers have been used to study the surface of Mars.*
Spanish cognate: robótico(a)

ACADEMIC GLOSSARY

ro•bot•ics
(roh-**bot**-iks)
noun the branch of technology that has to do with designing, building, and operating robots. *My brother is constructing an amazing programmable machine in a class on robotics.*
Origin: Latin *sect-*, meaning "cut off"
Spanish cognate: *robótica*

sec•tor
(**sek**-tur)
noun a part or division of a group. *The part of a country's economy that isn't controlled by the government is called the private sector.*
Origin: Latin *sect-*, meaning "cut off"
Spanish cognate: *sector*

sei•zure
(**see**-zhur)
noun a sudden attack of muscle contraction. *A problem in the brain's electrical activity can result in an epileptic seizure.*

se•ries
(**sihr**-eez)
noun a group of related things that follow in order. *This novel is the first in a series of stories that take place in ancient Egypt.*
Origin: Latin *serere*, meaning "join, connect"
Spanish cognate: *serie*

sim•i•lar
(**sim**-uh-lur)
adjective almost the same. *Both of these cars are bright red, but their color is the only way in which they are somewhat similar.*
Origin: Latin *similis*, meaning "like"
Spanish cognate: *similar*

so•cial
(**soh**-shuhl)
adjective having to do with the way people spend time and interact with other people. *Sometimes my parents refer to their friends as "our social circle."*
Origin: Latin *socius*, meaning "friend"
Spanish cognate: *social*

som•bre•ro
(som-**brer**-oh)
noun a tall, broad-brimmed hat, usually made of straw or felt, that is often worn in Mexico and the southwestern United States. *I wore a sombrero to keep the sun off my face.*
Origin: Latin *sub-*, meaning "under" + *umbra*, meaning "shade"
Spanish cognate: *sombrero*

sup•ply
(suh-**plye**)
noun an amount of something that is available for use. *Our teacher keeps a large supply of loose-leaf paper.*
Origin: Latin *supplere*, meaning "fill up"

symp•tom
(**simp**-tuhm)
noun something wrong with your body or mind that shows you are sick or hurt. *Your sneezing could be a symptom of a cold or an allergy.*
Origin: Greek *sumptōma*, meaning "chance, symptom"
Spanish cognate: *síntoma*

trans•late
(**transs**-late)
verb to result in. *Being well paid doesn't necessarily translate into becoming rich.*
Origin: Latin *translat-*, meaning "carried across"

trick
(**trik**)

1. *noun* something you do to deceive or surprise others. *If you try to play a trick on Aunt Jane, she won't be fooled—and she won't be happy.*
2. *verb* to deceive others or make them believe something that isn't true. *In this movie, the funny aliens trick a family into thinking that they are the family's long-lost relatives.*

trick•ster
(**trik**-stuhr)

noun a character who deceives or fools others, usually resulting in a victory over someone who is bigger and stronger. *In African folktales, the spider Anansi is a trickster; he often gets what he wants by fooling bigger animals.*

trick•y
(**trik**-ee)

adjective likely to use deception to get something. *That tricky child knows that if she pretends to cry, adults will do anything she wants in order to get her to stop.*

un•ac•cept•a•ble
(uhn-uhk-**sep**-tuh-buhl)

adjective not good enough to be allowed or agreed to. *Your idea is totally unacceptable to us; you'll have to figure out something else.*
Origin: Old English *un-*, meaning "not" + Latin *acceptare*, meaning "take or receive willingly," *-abilis*, meaning "able"
Spanish cognate: *inaceptable*

un•pre•dict•a•ble
(uhn-pri-**dik**-tuh-buhl)

adjective not able to know what a person will do next or what will happen next. *My baby sister is pretty unpredictable around strangers, so I can't tell you how she will act when you meet her.*
Origin: Old English *un-*, meaning "not" + Latin *prae-*, meaning "beforehand" + *dicere*, meaning "say," + *-abilis*, meaning "able"

val•u•a•ble
(**val**-yoo-uh-buhl)

adjective worth a lot of money or very useful in some other way. *Mr. Klein was surprised to learn that the autographed baseball he had been given as a child had become quite valuable.*
Origin: Latin *valere*, meaning "be worth" + *abilis*, meaning "able"
Spanish cognate: *valioso(a)*

wit
(**wit**)

noun the ability to say and do things that are clever. *Grandma's gentle wit makes everyone around her smile and feel comfortable.*

worth
(**wurth**)

adjective having a certain value in terms of money. *This ring is a fake, and it certainly is not worth the price you paid for it.*

SOURCES

Issue 1: Too Much Homework?

Fletcher, Bella and Elliott Hansing. "Homework Hubbub: Should Written Homework Be Banned on Weekends?" *WR News* 4-6 ed. 90.5 (2011): 3. Print.

Iasevoli, Brenda. "Rethinking Homework." *TIME for Kids (Grades 3-4)* 2.10 (2011): 4. Print.

Loveless, Tom. "Homework in America." Washington: The Brookings Institution. 18 Mar. 2014. Web. 25 Feb. 2015. <http://www.brookings.edu/research/reports/2014/03/18-homework-loveless>.

MetLife. "The MetLife Survey of the American Teacher: Teachers, Parents, and the Economy." MetLife Inc. Mar. 2012. Web. 25 Feb. 2015. <https://www.metlife.com/assets/cao/foundation/MetLife-Teacher-Survey-2011.pdf>.

"The Homework Hang-Up." *Weekly Reader News–Senior* 88.2 11 Nov. 2009: 3. Print.

Vatterott, Cathy. "Hints to Help Reduce Homework Stress." Alexandria: National PTA. 2014. Web. 25 Feb. 2015. <http://www.pta.org/content.cfm?ItemNumber=1730>.

Issue 2: Heads Up!

Centers for Disease Control and Prevention. "Nonfatal Traumatic Brain Injuries Related to Sports and Recreation Activities Among Persons Aged ≤ 19 Years – United States, 2001-2009." Atlanta: Centers for Disease Control and Prevention, 7 Oct. 2011. Web. 25 Feb. 2015. <http://www.cdc.gov/mmwr/preview/mmwrhtml/mm6039a1.htm>.

Gable, Lawrence. "The NFL Recognizes Players' Brain Damage." *What's Happening in the USA?* 21.6 (2014): 2. Print.

Graham, Robert, Frederick P. Rivara, Morgan A. Ford, and Carol Mason, Eds. "Sports-Related Concussions in Youth: Improving the Science, Changing the Culture." Washington: The National Academies Press, 2014. Print.

McCollum, Sean. "The Invisible Injury." *Scholastic Choices* 24.6 Apr.-May 2009: 1629. Print.

Modigliani, Laura. "Hard Knocks." *Scholastic News* 5/6 ed. 81.2 (2012): 4–5. Print.

The National Academies. *News From the National Academies.* Washington: The National Academies, 30 Oct. 2013. Web. 25 Feb. 2015. <http://www8.nationalacademies.org/onpinews/newsitem.aspx?RecordID=18377>.

National Conference of State Legislatures. "Traumatic Brain Injury Legislation." National Conference of State Legislatures, 28 July 2014. Web. 25 Feb. 2015. < http://www.ncsl.org/research/health/traumatic-brain-injury-legislation.aspx>.

Ouellette, John. "Is Heading Safe?" *Ayso.org.* American Youth Soccer Organization, 2015. Web. 25 Feb. 2015.

Safe Kids Worldwide. *Game Changers: Stats, Stories, and What Communities Are Doing to Protect Young Athletes.* Washington: Safe Kids Worldwide, Aug. 2013. Web. 25 Feb. 2015. <http://www.safekids.org/sites/default/files/documents/ResearchReports/game_changers__stats_stories_and_what_communites_are_doing_to_protect_young_athletes.pdf>.

Issue 3: Robo-Teachers

Asimov, Isaac. "The Fun They Had." *The Best of Isaac Asimov*. Garden City, NY: Doubleday, 1974. 153–156. Print.

Han, Jeong-Hye, et al. "Comparative Study on the Educational Use of Home Robots for Children." *Journal of Information Processing Systems* 4.4 (2008): 159–68. Korea Information Processing Society. Web. 23 Feb. 2015. PDF file. <http://jips-k.org/dlibrary/JIPS_v04_no4_paper5.pdf>.

"How RUBI Works." *Issues*. Vol. 2. New York: Scholastic, Inc. 2016. 24. Print.

Jango-Cohen, Judith. "My New Teacher, Mr. Robot." *SuperScience*. Scholastic, Nov.-Dec. 2010: 12–15. Print.

Price, Sean. "Get Ready for Robots." *National Geographic Kids*. National Geographic Society, Feb. 2013: 22–23. Print.

"Robotics: Facts." *Science Trek*. Idaho Public Television, n.d. Web. 23 Feb. 2015. <http://idahoptv.org/sciencetrek/topics/robots/facts.cfm>.

Smith, Aaron, and Janna Anderson. "AI, Robotics, and the Future of Jobs."*Pew Research Centers Internet American Life Project*. Pew Research Center, 06 Aug. 2014. Web. 11 Feb. 2015. <http://www.pewinternet.org/2014/08/06/future-of-jobs/>.

"VEX Robotics Competition—Toss Up." VEX Robotics, 31 May 2013. Web. 23 Feb. 2015. PDF file. <http://content.vexrobotics.com/docs/vex-toss-up/VEX-Toss-Up-GameManual_Rev053113.pdf>.

Issue 4: Learning to Code

Button, Becky. "Kids Can Code, No Problem." *NYTimes.com*. The New York Times Company, 12 May 2014. Web. 25 Feb. 2015.

Code.org. *Code.org*. Code.org, 2015. Web. 25 Feb. 2015.

Code.org. "Why Computer Science for Every Child?" Online video clip. *YouTube*. 4 Dec. 2013. Web. 25 Feb. 2014.

The College Board. AP Data — *Archived Data 2012*. New York: The College Board, 2012. Web. 25 Feb. 2015. <http://research.collegeboard.org/programs/ap/data/archived/2012>.

Dockterman, Eliana. "Cracking the Girl Code." *TimeforKids.com*. Time Inc., 1 Aug. 2014. Web. 25 Feb. 2015.

Dockterman, Eliana and Cameron Keady. "Cracking the Code." *TIME for Kids* (Grades 3–4) 5.5. New York: Scholastic, 2014. 4. Print.

Dvorak, John C. "Teaching Coding to Kids Is a Scam." *NYTimes.com*. The New York Times Company, 12 May 2014. Web. 25 Feb. 2014.

National Science Foundation. *Science and Engineering Indicators 2012*. Arlington: National Science Foundation, Jan. 2012. Web. 25 Feb. 2015. <http://www.nsf.gov/statistics/seind12/appendix.htm>.

SOURCES

Issue 4: Learning to Code (continued)

United States Dept. of Labor. Bureau of Labor Statistics. *Occupational Outlook Handbook: Computer Programmers*. Bureau of Labor Statistics, 8 Jan. 2014. Web. 25 Feb. 2015.

United States Dept. of Labor. Bureau of Labor Statistics. *U.S. Bureau of Labor Statistics*. Bureau of Labor Statistics. Web. 25 Feb. 2015.

Issue 5: Water Waste

"100+ Ways to Conserve." *Water Use It Wisely*. Water Use It Wisely, 25 Feb. 2015. Web. <http://wateruseitwisely.com/tips/category/kids/>.

"All Dry on the Western Front: Image of the Day." *Earth Observatory*. EOS Project Science Office, 23 Jan. 2014. Web. <http://earthobservatory.nasa.gov/IOTD/view.php?id=82910>.

"California Drought 2014: Farms." *California Drought 2014: Farm and Food Impacts*. United States Department of Agriculture, 12 Sept. 2014. Web. <http://ers.usda.gov/topics/in-the-news/california-drought-2014-farm-and-food-impacts/california-drought-2014-farms.aspx>.

"Drought Impact Study: California Agriculture Faces Greatest Water Loss Ever Seen." *UC Davis News & Information*. The Regents of the University of California, Davis Campus, 15 July 2014. Web. <http://news.ucdavis.edu/search/news_detail.lasso?id=10978>.

Gable, Lawrence. "Folsom Lake's Low Water Reveals Ruins." *What's Happening in California?* 15.7 (2014): 1. Print.

Jango-Cohen, Judith. "A Dwindling River." *Super Science* Oct. 2007: 6–9. Print.

Kraus, Stephanie. "Fines for Water-Wasters." *TIME for Kids*. Time, Inc., 16 July 2014. Web. <http://www.timeforkids.com/news/fines-water-wasters/167311>.

Sullivan, Justin. 2014. Getty Images, Oroville, CA.

"U.S. Drought Monitor Map Archive." *U.S. Drought Monitor*. The National Integrated Drought Information System. Web. <http://droughtmonitor.unl.edu/MapsAndData/MapArchive.aspx>.

"Where is the drought? Will it change? What are its impacts?" *U.S. Drought Portal*. The National Integrated Drought Information System. Web. <http://www.drought.gov/drought/>.

Issue 6: Trickster Tales

"About Barbara Winther." Barbara Winther. 2015. Web. <http://www.barbarawinther.com/>.

Brothers Grimm. "Little Red Cap." Trans. Edgar Taylor and Marian Edwardes. *The Project Gutenberg EBook of Grimms' Fairy Tales*. Project Gutenberg, 14 Dec. 2008. Web. <http://www.gutenberg.org/files/2591/2591-h/2591-h.htm>.

Dahl, Roald. "Little Red Riding Hood and the Wolf." *Revolting Rhymes*. New York: Penguin Group, 1982. 36–40. Print.

Winther, Barbara. "Pedro's Holey Sombrero." *Plays from Hispanic Tales*. Boston: Plays, 1998. 76–81. Print.

Wong, B. D., Ernest V. Troost, and Ed Young. *Lon Po Po: a Red Riding Hood Story From China*. Norwalk, CT: Weston Woods, 2006.

CREDITS

ISSUE 1: TOO MUCH HOMEWORK?

ISSUE 2: HEADS UP!

ISSUE 3: ROBO-TEACHERS

ISSUE 4: LEARNING TO CODE

ISSUE 5: WATER WASTE

CREDITS